24: Military Lessons of the Yom Kippur War: Historical Perspectives

330082

THE WASHINGTON PAPERS
Volume III

24: Military Lessons of the Yom Kippur War: Historical Perspectives

Martin van Creveld

THE CENTER FOR STRATEGIC AND INTERNATIONAL STUDIES
Georgetown University, Washington, D.C.

SAGE PUBLICATIONS
Beverly Hills / London

Copyright © 1975 by
The Center for Strategic and International Studies
Georgetown University

Printed in the United States of America

All rights reserved. No part of this book may be reproduced
or utilized in any form or by any means, electronic or mechanical,
including photocopying, recording, or by any
information storage and retrieval system, without permission in writing
from the publisher.

For information address:

SAGE PUBLICATIONS, INC.
275 South Beverly Drive
Beverly Hills, California 90212

SAGE PUBLICATIONS LTD
St George's House / 44 Hatton Garden
London EC1N 8ER

International Standard Book Number 0-8039-0562-9

Library of Congress Catalog Card No. 75-13845

FIRST PRINTING

When citing a Washington Paper, please use the proper form. Remember to cite the series title and include the paper number. One of the two following formats can be adapted (depending on the style manual used):

(1) HASSNER, P. (1973) "Europe in the Age of Negotiation." The Washington Papers, I, 8. Beverly Hills and London: Sage Pubns.

OR

(2) Hassner, Pierre. 1973. *Europe in the Age of Negotiation.* The Washington Papers, vol. 1, no. 8. Beverly Hills and London: Sage Publications.

CONTENTS

	Introduction	vii
I.	Background and Theory	1
II.	The War in Outline	11
III.	The Lessons	21
	The Weapons	22
	Tactics, or the Character of Battle	32
	Strategy, or the Character of War	39
IV.	Perspectives	47
	Notes	51
	References	56
	Map of Israel-Egypt Agreement	58
	The Agreement	60

INTRODUCTION

Since the end of World War II, large-scale weapon production has tended to concentrate around, and to be destined for, presumed battlefields in Central Europe. The United States, the Soviet Union, and their allies: these, with the important but unhelpful exception of Japan, are the only powers still capable of producing the ultimate in military hardware. Except for the United States, however, none of them has been engaged in large-scale warfare during the last quarter of a century; and even the American experience in Vietnam was limited mainly to antiguerrilla operations waged under conditions little relevant to those that would obtain in a large-scale armed clash between fully modern powers.

There have been, it is true, some partial exceptions to the above situation. The Korean War of 1950-1953 was fought on a considerable scale but did not, as far as weapons were concerned, go much beyond World War II. The Suez campaign of 1956 was very instructive at the time, but is now almost twenty years past. The Indian—Pakistani wars of 1965 and 1971 were comparatively modern affairs but took place over terrain of such appalling difficulty as to render any more general application hazardous. Most other wars were smallish conflicts waged between or against peoples totally unequipped for modern warfare. The result of this lack of experience was that the battlefields for which the main weapon-producing powers designed their arms became increasingly hypothetical; and discussion in professional literature only serves to underline the fact that nobody really knows what a full-scale modern war, even one waged with conventional weapons, will be like.

On the face of it, the Six Days War—the third round in the Arab-Israeli conflict, fought in 1967—had more to offer by the way of lessons. Here, at last, was a war between states that, if hardly representing the acme of modernity, did at least possess arms supplied by the main weapon-producing countries on a very considerable scale. However, even in this case the modernity was more apparent than real. Despite the presence of many T-54s and T-55s, in the Egyptian tank force there were still many T-34s and JS-IIIs. The Syrians even numbered German Mark IV tanks (1936 vintage) among their armor, together with many more T-34s and T-54s, while the Israelis used the so-called "Super Sherman" (with improved engines and 90 mm. gun) as well as more modern M-48s and Centurions. Centurion and half track, bazooka and recoilless rifle—all were taken straight out of World War II.

Since both the Israelis and their opponents used World War II weapons, Israel also waged a World War II style campaign. As some observers noted at the time, the Six Days' War was taken straight out of the pages of Heinz Guderian, creator of the German armored force. It was as if a time machine had turned the clock back by a quarter of a century; was it not in 1939-1941 that a handful of Panzer divisions used their speed and mobility to overrun one country after the other? Even as World War II progressed, however, such campaigns became increasingly rare. Attempts to mount them were broken up by heavily fortified defensive belts—as at Kursk—in the east, and by the dominance of Allied airpower in the west. Hence, it would be no exaggeration to say that the Six Days' War was old-fashioned not only in its own time but even in terms of the later years of World War II.

Not so the fourth Arab-Israeli round, commonly known as the Yom Kippur War. Here at last was a conflict that, though still falling short of the ultimate in modern arms, at least came very close to it. While some of the weapons in question were very much out of date—such as the American-built half track used by the Israelis—others, such as the guided antitank and antiaircraft missiles employed by the Arabs, were so new as to appear for the first time ever. Both sides, too, possessed these weapons on a scale unrivaled since the largest battles of World War II. For these reasons, this war is likely to be studied for some time and has many significant lessons to offer.

How such lessons should be derived is, methodologically, a difficult problem. Obviously, any attempt to learn from historical events must start with an effort to separate the grain from the chaff, the universal from the localized, the permanent from the accidental. Taking for example the two wars discussed above, were the differences between them due to such "accidental" causes as the disregarding of this or that piece of intelligence, the incompetence of this or that general, or the respective qualities of the armies involved? If so, history should confine itself to a narrative of events. If, however, there are deeper factors at work, going beyond these and similar accidents peculiar to one time and one place; if historical method is available to help identify those factors; in that case, history may have significant lessons to offer.

The problem, then, is where to draw the line separating the "accidental" from the permanent. Since the present study aims less at drawing an approximate picture of the next Arab-Israeli round than at assessing the long-term significance of the Yom Kippur War for warfare as a whole, we shall assume that the factor common to all theaters of war is military technology. Of course, the presence or absence of this or that weapon on any given battlefield is itself "accidental"; nevertheless, the assumption is justified in so far as all wars are nowadays waged with weapons designed more or less for the central European battlefield. We shall therefore assume that, more than any other factor, it is arms technology that nowadays determines the character, not of this or that war but of war in general. It is here that the lessons most capable of a wider application are to be found.

However, a mere enumeration of technological developments, past, present, and future, is insufficient. In any case, a detailed inquiry of this kind is far beyond the capacity of this writer. What we are seeking is some kind of indication, not merely of the shape of future weapons but of the way those weapons will affect those elusive qualities, the "character" of battle, the "fare" behind war. Here military history may help because, as we shall try to show, it presents some patterns that repeat themselves.

To define these patterns, some theory of warfare is absolutely essential. Having studied many such theories, the writer is aware of their limitations; no theory will ever be able to embrace all the facts, much less explain them. Moreover, the concept of "warfare" itself, though indispensable for any comparison, is to some extent misleading. It rests on the assumption that the wars of each period and place, each stage of civilization, have some more or less well-defined "character" made up by the sum of the methods used to fight them. In reality, of course, every armed encounter is to a large extent *sui generis*. Still, almost any theory is preferable to none at all. Without theory, as Clausewitz (1962) says, no understanding is possible; indeed, the very concept of understanding becomes meaningless. The uniqueness of historical events does not prevent us from speaking about "the spirit of the Renaissance" or "nineteenth century economics"; surely, therefore, it should not exclude such concepts as "Napoleonic" or "modern" warfare. Such concepts, while undoubtedly representing crude generalizations, nevertheless have their use in our attempts to explore the relationship between those periods and the ones preceeding or succeeding them.

If military history is to be of any use beyond a mere narrative of past conflicts, its task should consist, first, of defining the terms of reference by which war is to be described; second, of describing the specific war in question as well as possible within those terms; and finally, of an attempt to explain why that particular form of war was customary at that time and that place, how it differed from what went before, and what reasons caused it to fall into abeyance at a later date.

This, then, will be the outline followed by the present study. Written at a time when war may recur again, its conclusions must necessarily be of a tentative nature; and in any case, its aim is not to draw an approximate picture of the next Arab-Israeli boxing match but to try and isolate those aspects of the Yom Kippur War that, rather than being due to "accidental" factors peculiar to that war, stem from deeper causes and would thus appear to be relevant to the future of conventional war in general. To this purpose, we shall first try to create an encompassing framework by working out some basic relationships that seem useful toward the understanding of events; second, to use that framework in order to describe the Yom Kippur War to the best of our ability and the sources at our command; and finally, to ask how and why this war differed from the ones preceding it, and what can be deduced from this difference about the direction in which modern war is moving. The above procedure is a difficult one to follow; nevertheless, it seems to the author the only one capable of producing results. Whether, in fact, this is so remains for the reader to judge.

I. BACKGROUND AND THEORY

The fifth of June, 1967, was one of the most fateful days in the history of the State of Israel. After three weeks of tense expectation, there arrived at 0815 hours of that day in the headquarters of Major General Yeshajahu Gavish, CIC Southern Front, a curt and cryptic message: *"Sadin Adom"* (red sheet), the prearranged signal for the start of Israel's preemptive attack on Egypt. Within minutes, thousands of vehicle engines all along the Israeli-Egyptian border roared into life; camouflage nets were swiftly discarded, and with three Israeli divisions storming forward it looked, in the words of a pilot overflying the scene, as if the whole frontier had suddenly started moving westward in a huge cloud of dust.

The right flank of the Israeli array, stretching along the border from a point roughly opposite Gaza in a southwesterly direction for about thirty miles, was formed by a division-sized task force (a so-called *Ugda*) consisting of two armored brigades with perhaps 250-300 tanks and a brigade of paratroopers on half tracks. Commanding this elite force was Major General Israel Tal, a tough, aggressive personality who served as Director of Israel's Armoured Corps and seemed ideally suited to the task now facing him; namely, in his own words, that of carrying out the decisive trial of strength designed not only to open the way into the Sinai but, above all, to establish the Israeli Defence Forces' (IDF) moral superiority over an enemy with whom they had not clashed for over ten years (Young, 1967: 104).

If this, in fact, was the division's task, it was carried out in masterly fashion. Fighting, to quote Tal again, a "brutal battle," the bulk of the *Ugda* attacked the opposing forces—the Egyptian Seventh Division and the Palestinian Twentieth Division, the latter in brigade strength—head on and succeeded in breaking through the deep, strongly fortified positions centering around Khan Yunis, Rafa, and the Jerardi defile on the coastal road to El Arish. It was a tough battle that cost the Israelis extremely heavy casualties—thirty-five tank commanders are said to have been killed during the advance on Khan Yunis alone—but it did achieve its purpose; at midnight, though isolated Egyptian pockets continued to hold out all along the way back to the Israeli border, the town of El Arish—some forty miles from the original starting positions—had been reached by the spearhead of Tal's division. This was Colonel Shmuel Gonen's Seventh Armoured Brigade, which was destined to crown a classic tank-cum-aircraft Blitzkrieg by being the first unit to reach the Suez Canal just 48 hours later.

The "Battle of Rafah," as Tal's advance came to be known in Israel, was commonly regarded as the toughest fight of the entire Six Days' War. It gave rise to many solemn anniversaries and to at least one popular song. Those who had fought "exposed in the turrets"[2] became the subjects of a hero cult; the men who had led the charge—primarily Gonen and Tal himself—were henceforward marked men, clearly destined for higher command. Above all, the battle had far-reaching effects in that it molded Israeli thought about the shape of the next war. The fact that Tal had modified his tactics on the second day of the war was overlooked; taking a leaf out of John Frederick Fuller, terms like "armored might" and "armored shock" became household words in Israel, denoting an almost mystical faith in the tank and its ability to move quickly, strike hard, and sweep any other kind of troops clean off the battlefield. Armor, which had already occupied a central place in Israel's array of battle, now became the recognized "queen of the battlefield" designed to replace or at least absorb all other arms. Fighting was declared to be "90 percent technics and 10 percent tactics"; accordingly, future wars were conceived in terms of massive frontal clashes between tank armies which, once victory had been won through the superior quality of Israel's tankmen, would be followed by a campaign of maneuver deep into the rear of an already defeated enemy. An army that had traditionally put its trust in subtlety and the indirect approach (see Yadin, 1954) now came to regard the frontal armored charge as the acme of tactics; organized in their own separate corps and trained in their own separate schools, tank men were taught to look down on other arms and came to regard their participation or even presence on the battlefield as an unnecessary encumbrance that would merely slow down what was known as "armored pace."

As the years went by, more details about the events of the Six Days' War gradually became known and began to modify the picture.[3] It now appeared that the Battle of Rafah, though hard fought and well won, had hardly been a masterpiece of military art. Tal, it became clear, had jeopardized his *Ugda* by failing to control the movements of his brigade commanders, some of whom went off on wild goose chases of their own and subsequently found themselves cut off. Coordination between the different arms—particularly tanks and half tracks—had been faulty, leading to many unnecessary casualties. Individual units had become stuck in the dunes, had run out of fuel, or simply had got lost and out of control. If the battle was initially believed to have been fought against the cream of Egypt's army, it now transpired that the troops involved were second grade. Above all, the whole bloody affair had originated in a tankman's arrogant confidence in the ability of his troops to break through "regardless of cost"; had Tal been content to wait for the Israeli Air Force (IAF) to finish its task of destroying the Egyptian Air Force, the planes might well have cleared the way in front of his tanks and made the battle much easier if not altogether unnecessary.

While history was thus busy modifying the accepted picture of the battle, warning voices concerning the feasibility of a repeat performance were also raised. To list but two out of a great many examples, there appeared in 1970 a book (Orgill, 1970: 256-257) that not only dared to question the future of the tank but also went so far as to call Israel's 1967 victory an old-fashioned campaign. A year later Ferdinand Miksche (1971), a well-known military critic and expert on armor, published an article in which he cast doubts on the tank's ability to get through a well-defended front in any future war. Both warnings were registered in Israel, and a good part of the 1971-1972 (23-26) issues of *Bema'arahot Shirjon* (*Armoured Arrays,* the now defunct Israeli Tank Corps Journal) was devoted to discussing them. The tenor of the argument can readily be divined from such titles as "The Galloping Corpse" and "The Tank, King of the Battlefield"; thus, in spite of mounting historical evidence to the contrary and professional skepticism abroad, the IDF's belief in the tank phalanx, armored shock, and Blitzkrieg as its *ultima ratio* persisted.

Three Essential Elements. Throughout history, all combat can be said to have consisted of three essential elements, namely, striking power, mobility, and protection. Striking power to hit and incapacitate one's enemy; movement to reach or, if necessary, escape him; protection to save oneself from injury while engaged in the other two; it is the combination of these basic principles that has made up the armed encounter from times immemorial and will presumably always continue to do so.

If the principles of striking, moving, and protecting have remained constant throughout the fifty-odd centuries of warfare about which something is known, the *means* utilized to translate them into practice have undergone immense and horrible development. To hit their enemies, men invented weapons ranging from the primeval club to the most recent guided missile. To reach or escape their foes, they employed increasingly complex techniques of locomotion from walking to flying. To protect themselves, they began by climbing up a tree and ended up (for the time being) by enclosing themselves in reinforced concrete and armor plate. In between these extremes of primitivism and modernism, the number of variations originated has been very large indeed.

In view of the almost unbelievable ingenuity displayed by man in his endless quest for improved striking power, mobility, and protection, it is surprising that, throughout recorded history, the fundamental methods by which he struck, moved, and protected himself have remained not only constant but very few in number. Thus, in order to obtain protection, a body of troops can do one of two things. It can try to withstand hostile striking power by interposing some kind of movable screen or armor between itself and the enemy; or it can try to avoid this striking power by either taking cover, or remaining dispersed, or keeping in motion.

In the same way, movement on the battlefield can be carried out in one of two aboriginal forms. To close with its enemy, an army may move in a phalanx—a dense, tight formation distinguished by considerable depth and by the rigidity with which its individual members are subordinated to the whole. On the other end of the scale, troops may move in a loose, thin, and flexible formation; in the most extreme case this will give rise to a formless swarm of skirmishers and storm parties whose very essence is the complete absence of any attempt to tie the movements of one man to those of another.

Finally, striking power may also be divided into two basic categories. Normally, the side enjoying superior strength or numbers will do its best to close with the enemy; this means close combat weapons, reliance on weight, and shock action. By contrast, the weaker party must endeavor to keep the enemy at arm's length; to this end he will trust to devices hurled from afar, entailing fire or missile power.

The Master Principle. Since striking, moving, and protecting make up combat, all historical armed encounters could be classified as well as described in terms of the dominant methods used to achieve them. To the extent that war is a series of armed encounters, the general character of any specific war could also be defined in the same way. To do so, however, is a complicated business, and students of military history have usually tried to avoid it by selecting one of the three as a "master principle" and concentrating on the methods used to achieve it. The criteria according to which this selection was made generally had absolutely nothing to do with historical method. Thus, Tom

Wintringham (1943: 21-37) frankly admits that he chose protection for no better reason that "because I am British," then proceeds to divide history into "armored" and "unarmored" periods succeeding each other cyclically. Another and greater writer (Fuller, 1936a: 227-229) did not feel his Britishness made him essentially protective by nature; as the apostle of that supreme striking instrument that is the tank, he constructed a system under which striking power, regarded as the master-principle, was used to divide history into periods based on shock actions as opposed to those based on firepower. In the same way, it should be possible—if, indeed, it has not been done already—to divide all wars according to whether movement on the battlefield was carried out in close order or in an open one.

That the above-mentioned systems are, taken separately, inadequate is suggested not only by the fact that combat is necessarily made up of all three principles, but also because the periods into which they divide the history of war as a whole are remarkably similar. Battles such as Marathon (490 B.C.), Adrianople (378 A.D.), Pavia (774), Hastings (1066), Crecy (1346), Valmy (1792), and Cambrai (1917), figure prominently in most, if not all, books on military history. This is due, not merely to coincidence or to the politically decisive results of these battles (as battles, in fact, many of them were not decisive), but to their being taken for historical turning points in the sense that they witnessed a significant and permanent change in the combination of methods by which the three principles were put into practice.

Military history, then, can be divided into periods according to the dominant combination or combinations of methods used to strike, move, and protect at any given time; a shift from one period to the next is marked by the victory of one combination over another as manifested by some "decisive battle." The question as to which particular combination is used at each time and place obviously depends on such "accidental" factors as the task at hand, the terrain, and the enemy against whom one's efforts are directed; furthermore, armed encounters may be divided into distinct stages (such as initial clash, main action, and mopping-up operations) each calling for a different combination and, consequently, for a different kind of troops.[4]

Behind these factors, which are peculiar to each individual battlefield, however, there are certain principles governing the combinations of methods that may be employed. The first of these is the need to pay attention to all three of them, a problem made more difficult by the fact that each can ultimately be increased only at the expense of the others. To achieve greater striking power, a soldier may well have to carry a heavier weapon which, inevitably, will interfere with his mobility and possibly with his ability to defend himself. Though individual men may theoretically possess a greater freedom of movement than a more or less compact body, they may have to sacrifice part of their mobility in order to obtain protection by sticking together. A fortress, to give a final example, is basically nothing but a form of protection carried so far as to sacrifice virtually all possibility of movement. An army's ability to select a particular means of striking, moving, and protecting is thus limited by the need to pay attention to the other two principles; failure to do so is to court disaster.

Secondly, a close look at the history of war suggests that the various methods by which men have sought to achieve striking power, mobility, and protection are positively interrelated. In all ages and regardless of the state of technology, reliance on shock action for striking has meant armor for protection and a close order in movement. The use of fire as the main method for hitting one's enemy, on the other hand, invariably led to armor being diminished or even discarded in favor of either cover, or dispersion, or fast movement. If shock action necessarily entails mobility in order to close with one's foe, firepower has often paralyzed movement on the battlefield and sometimes ended up by also eliminating the possibility of strategic movement from one battlefield to another. Thus, a tactical or technological innovation leading to a change in the methods used to achieve any one principle was invariably followed by corresponding changes in the methods used to achieve the other two, although, armies being "temples of ancestor worship" (Basil Liddell Hart), the change often took a long time and a string of terrible defeats to materialize.[5]

Since the number of methods utilized to carry out the basic principles of combat is so small, and as even this small number shows a definite tendency to appear only in certain combinations and not in others, it should come as no surprise that the patterns of warfare have often repeated themselves throughout the ages. Thus, for example, there is a clear resemblance between the clashes of medieval knights and modern tank warfare because both rely on shock action for striking (even when, in the case of the tank, the shock action is produced by firepower weapons, a seemingly paradoxical statement the meaning of which will be made clear below), armor for protection, and a comparatively close order while moving at high speed.[6] The Swiss pike formation of the fourteenth and fifteenth centuries bore a strong resemblance to the Macedonian phalanx; both employed a single tremendous shock for striking, an extremely close order in movement, and armor for protection (to be exact, it should be added that the two formations differed in that the Swiss were less ready to sacrifice speed for armor). Both were eventually overcome by troops wearing heavier armor, relying on a series of small shocks for striking, and moving in a somewhat more flexible order—the Roman legions and the Spanish sword-and-buckler men.[7] Given this tendency of the forms of war to repeat themselves, it is possible to foresee the future results of any development in the methods employed to carry through one of the three basic principles with some degree of certainty.

Needless to say, these results are not limited to the effects of the three principles on each other. Rather, they extend to other aspects of the military art; weapons necessarily affect tactics and these have often determined strategy. Furthermore, the shift from one combination to another affects the relationship between defense and offense, attrition and annihilation; indirectly, it also influences the relationship between strategy[8] and the wider aspects of policy. While it would be too much to claim that all these factors repeat themselves cyclically, there are, I believe, certain more general trends associated with each kind of period as determined by the particular combination of methods for striking, moving, and protecting employed.

Two important reservations should be made here. First, terms such as "close combat," "long range," a "close order," or a "flexible formation" are relative. Compared to the long-range artillery duels of the early years of World War I, tank warfare as it developed after 1917 was carried out at close quarters, although this did not of course entail a reversion to medieval hand-to-hand combat.[9] Similarly, the armored phalanxes that broke through the opposing lines in Poland, France, and Russia during the early years of World War II were much more tightly grouped than, say, the lines of skirmishers that fought the wars of the late nineteenth century, although they were far from being as closely packed as the original Macedonian phalanx. Thus, though periods of close and long-range combat, rigid formations and flexible ones, succeed each other cyclically, history as a whole shows a definite tendency toward longer and longer ranges and looser and looser formations.

Second, it should be noted that most historical periods were, in fact, times of transition in the sense that reliance for striking, moving, and protecting was placed not on any single method but on a combination of several ones. Since the number of "accidental" factors that has to be considered when determining the methods to be used is very large, commanders of all ages have striven to build—balance is the correct word—their forces in such a way as to enable them to adapt to circumstances in the sense of employing more than one combination of methods. This balancing may be achieved in one of two ways: either by training and arming each individual soldier in such a manner as to enable him to meet the maximum number of contingencies, or by dividing the force into arms, each employing one particular combination of methods to suit one particular task or set of circumstances. Thus, the Greek hoplites—heavy infantry using shock for striking, armor for protection, and a close order in movement—were sometimes accompanied by peltasts, or light troops, relying on firepower (bows and arrows, slings, javelins) for striking, light or no armor for protection, and a loose order in movement (see Adcock, 1957: 14-29). To give another example, both Napoleon's infantry and his cavalry fell into "light" and "heavy" types distinguished by the different methods they used to hit, move, and protect themselves (see Chandler, 1966: 332-336). Given the fact that each of these arms will be at its best under one particular set of circumstances, victory may often turn on the correct selection of their proportion to each other.

In actual fact, due to the above considerations, armies relying exclusively on any one method to carry through each of the three principles have been comparatively rare, though not unknown, and were usually beaten by troops relying on several such combinations.[10] This is an important point, for it serves to remind us that the above discussion is no more than an attempt to create a conceptual framework by listing the extremes of each method used; practice, by contrast, has usually hovered between those extremes or, alternatively, combined them.

King Tank. Having come so far, we can now turn our minds back to the Yom Kippur War. Following its 1967 victory, Israel entered that war with a military doctrine centering around a firm belief in one particular combination of methods for carrying out the basic principles of combat. Technically, this belief found its symbol in "The Tank, King of the Battlefield"; tactically, it could be summed up by awe-inspiring shock, "armored shock," carried out by a mighty phalanx of armored fighting vehicles; strategically, it was expected to pierce the enemy front and lead to another Blitzkrieg shorter even than the Six Days' War. How did these beliefs emerge out of the fog of war? Assuming that history can be divided into periods according to the dominant methods used for carrying out the three basic principles of combat, has a shift taken place? And if so, what is the significance of this for the future? These are the questions that, on the basis of a preliminary examination of the course of events, the present study will try to answer.

II. THE WAR IN OUTLINE

Looking down upon the Sinai desert on the evening of October 7, 1973, an airborne observer trained to think in terms of "classic" armored warfare—the kind of campaign that had won Israel her lightning victory in the very same area only six years earlier—would scarcely have believed his eyes. What was going on below had little to do with that kind of war; nor did it have much in common with war as envisaged by Egypt's presumed Soviet mentors or, for that matter, with most kinds of war as it has been waged during the last 50-odd years.[11]

Perhaps the biggest surprise of all was the composition of the force that had crossed the Suez Canal since the war began 36 hours earlier. Normally, one would expect a small number of specialist troops to start the crossing, to be followed by no more infantry than are needed to more or less secure the initial bridgeheads. Next, it would be the task of the armored troops to extend those bridgeheads as rapidly as possible, with motorized infantry and artillery following up in order to eliminate such resistance as may have escaped the attention of the tanks, and to consolidate the latter's gains.

In fact, nothing of this kind took place. The elite sapper units that had first crossed the Canal and pierced the embankment protecting the Israeli side were not followed by any significant quantity of armor but by huge masses of infantry on foot, and then more of the same—coming on "like ants,"[12] until there were some 70,000 of them, divided between two armies[13] whose junction line was just north of the Great Bitter Lake. Only at a later stage—four or five days after the initial crossings—was the infantry reinforced by strong armored tanks, while such tanks as had accompanied the infantry were used to reduce strongholds rather than to spearhead the advance. In any case, much of the Egyptian tank forces, numbering approximately 2,000 vehicles,[14] remained on the west side of the Canal right up to the end of the war.

Tactically and strategically, the Egyptian stroke was also unorthodox. Disregarding most precedents, General Ahmed Ismail's troops did not concentrate their blows against a few selected points; rather, apparently in the hope of forcing the IAF to disperse its efforts, they threw their bridges over the 100-mile Canal along its entire length from Port Said to Suez. Having gained a foothold on the eastern bank and having overcome or isolated the Israeli strongholds on the water line, they did not try to advance much deeper into the Sinai; instead of thrusting eastward with open flanks, as Soviet military doctrine would dictate, they flexed their elbows north and south in order to eliminate any gaps and make their bridgehead continuous. Only at a later stage did they start a drive eastward, but even so it was a slow, methodical affair making little use of speed or maneuver and seemingly more concerned with securing its own flanks than with seizing as large a part of the Sinai as possible before the Israeli reserves, streaming westward all over the northern half[15] of the Peninsula, arrived to contain them.[16] By the end of the second day, the Egyptians had still not advanced more than six to ten miles inland from the Canal—a surprising fact, for lack of coordination had caused the initial counterattacks mounted by such regular forces as Israel kept in the Sinai to fail and there was little to prevent the victorious Egyptians from penetrating further on.[17]

The air force, that instrument par excellence of all modern attackers, was conspicuous only by its absence. In 1939 and again in 1940 and 1941, the Germans opened their offensives against Poland, France, and the Soviet Union with a shattering air strike; so did the Japanese at Pearl Harbor and, of course, the Israelis in 1967. These and other experiences led to the almost universal belief, fully shared by the Israeli Intelligence Service (see the Agranat Inquiry Commission's Report, 1974), that no large-scale offensive could succeed in face of enemy superiority in the air. The Egyptians, however, proved the contrary by crossing the Canal with no kind of air cover except that provided by ground defenses; they did, to be sure, drop some bombs on the Bar Lev Line and on targets farther to the rear, but on the whole the 600-plane Egyptian air force remained remarkably inactive.[18] Not so the hitherto invincible IAF, whose F-4 Phantoms and A-4 Skyhawks are reported to have gone into action within 26 minutes of the initial crossings but whose desperate attempts to destroy the bridges thrown over the Canal were being frustrated by the murderous fire of antiaircraft missiles and, when they tried to avoid those by flying at low altitudes, by that of four-barrelled ZSU-23 cannon spitting out ammunition at the rate of 4,000 rounds a minute.

Against the Egyptian advance, the Israelis had only very inadequate forces immediately available. The Bar Lev Line, consisting of 35 strongholds on the water line and another 12 or so some miles to the rear, was manned by only 25 percent of the personnel for which it had been designed and may even have been in the process of a last minute evacuation.[19] Two armored brigades—with perhaps 280 tanks all told—were stationed at Bir Gafgafa, some 50 miles to the rear, and thus took several hours to come into action.[20] Once committed, they failed to concentrate their efforts but operated in penny packets all along the front, their task being made more difficult by the fact that the eastern (Israeli) bank of the Canal was dominated by the massive earthen ramparts erected on the western side.[21] By the evening of Sunday, October 7, the Bar Lev Line had been overrun and the forces supporting it reduced to a fraction of their original strength.

The biggest surprise of all, however, was still to come. True, the initial counterattacks had failed; nevertheless, the GOC South, Major General Shmuel Gonen, could still console himself with the hope that, once Israel's reserves came into action, their counterattack would wipe the Egyptians clean off the map. By the morning of October 8, these forces had arrived and were deploying; the Israelis, as one soldier put it to me, expected the armored charges to go "like a knife through butter." So great was their confidence that the tankmen were frankly nonplussed by the fact that the Egyptian infantry, instead of running at the first sight of armor (as foot soldiers have been expected to do ever since Hitler's Panzers knifed through the Polish army in 1939) stood fast and held their ground (Insight Team, 1973). This fact, however, did not cause them to halt and think, as perhaps it should have. Blindly, as it seems now, they charged forward, with the result that when the smoke cleared the attacking forces had been smashed to bits by a hail of antitank missiles.[22] Here, plain for all to see, was a historic turning point; the tank, a shock weapon par excellence that had stood out as the very symbol of armed might during the last 50 years, had finally met its match in the form of a novel device based on firepower.[23]

Slugging Match on the Golan Heights. Meanwhile, on the Golan Heights, the picture was not dissimilar although the roles were to some extent reversed. The Syrians, unlike their Egyptian brethren, adhered fairly closely to the Soviet military doctrine that envisages conventional war in terms of a super Blitzkrieg; accordingly, they did not spread out their forces in a clear and deliberate advance but instead tried to engage in mobile warfare and engage a classic four-pronged pincer movement. Eight hundred tanks and 28,000 mechanized infantry advanced across terrain in parade ground fashion; shortly, however, they ran into trouble in the face of ferocious Israeli resistance. Though heavily outnumbered, the Israelis used such armor as they had immediately available to the best effect, shooting from prepared positions and weaving interlocking fields of fire. By sheer weight of numbers, the Syrians broke through; nevertheless, they apparently suffered such heavy casualties that, on the second day, they modified their tactics and tried to imitate the Egyptians by advancing in line abreast. In doing so they ran afoul of the Israeli Air Force, which was by now almost the only effective force defending the Golan and whose planes, though losing heavily to antiaircraft fire, flew in low from the south over Jordanian territory and took them in the flank.

By Monday morning, the Israeli reserves were beginning to arrive in force whereas the Syrians, despite an initial five to one superiority in tanks and an even greater advantage in infantry and antitank weapons, had still not advanced more than ten miles into the Golan.[24] Here, as in the Sinai, the lesson was clear. On both fronts, the attempts of both sides to use armor for shock in order to achieve a tactical breakthrough followed by strategic penetration into the rear had failed in front of troops relying on firepower. In the Sinai, that firepower had been produced—albeit at an enormous cost in human lives—by infantry carrying guided weapons; in the Golan, given the fact that Israel lacked any significant quantity of antitank weapons,[25] the tanks themselves had served in the role of antitank guns.

From Monday onward, fighting on the Golan Heights developed into a confused slugging match, "stalking warfare" that gave little scope to strategy or even grand tactics in the usual sense. On neither side was there much attempt to gain an advantage by maneuver; instead, there took place a shooting match that the Israelis, being much the better shots,[26] were apt to win. By the end of the week they were clearly doing just that; Israeli mechanized infantry, covered by artillery and tanks and strongly supported from the air,[27] was on its way to Damascus. The Syrians had lost about 1,000 tanks,[28] including those that had been sent in on Thursday, October 11, in a desperate counterattack. The war, however, differed from the previous ones in that many of those tanks had been destroyed in combat, and only comparatively few were abandoned by crews as a result of finding themselves isolated miles behind the front. It was a victory, a great one even; still, in the words of one Israeli commander (quoted by Insight Team, 1973: 102), it had not been "our sort of war." In particular, the predominance of firepower on the battlefield had restricted tactical maneuver, and consequently no quick or elegant victories were won. Instead, it had been a brutal war of attrition; a *materialschlacht* on a huge scale that left both sides bruised and bleeding.

In this war, there had been little or no attempt at strategic maneuver; an army such as the IDF, which has traditionally (at any rate, until 1967) relied on finesse and the "indirect approach" to achieve its ends, could perhaps have been expected to devise a better means to gain victory than launching a purely frontal attack along the shortest, but also topographically most difficult, road to Damascus. Whether or not a more indirect approach, such as an advance on the extreme southern flank between Syria and Jordan with an eye to encircling the Syrian army,[29] was possible and would have produced better results is still a moot point and will not be known for certain until the Israeli (and Syrian) archives are opened, that is *ad Kalendas Grecas*. As it was, General David Elazar (1973) had promised "to break their bones"; he ended up by doing just that, although the process remained incomplete and resulted in not a few bones being broken on the Israeli side, too.

More disturbing even than the lack of finesse in the IDF's operational conduct of the war against Syria was the apparent absence of a coherent strategy. The Israeli decision to tackle Syria first, apparently made early in if not before the war, resulted from the proximity of the fighting to her centers of population and was also designed to deter Jordan from entering the war (see Dayan, 1974b); as such, it was fundamentally correct. However, the question remains why the Israelis went over to the offensive after having repulsed the Syrian offensive. Given the nature and direction of the advance they can hardly have hoped to deliver a knock-out blow; nor, it must have been clear, would political considerations allow them to enter Damascus. Granted that no decisive victory could reasonably be expected to follow from an advance into Syria, its only justification was presumably the wish to break as many Syrian (and Iraqi, and Jordanian) bones as possible; an aim which, it cannot be denied, was admirably carried out.

Stalemate in the Sinai. While the two sides were engaged in their slugging match in Syria, something of a stalemate had developed in the Sinai. Having suffered a material and psychological shock, Israel launched no further counterattacks to dislodge the Egyptian foothold on the Canal; the arrival on Wednesday of former COS Haim Bar Lev to take over command also heralded a new and chastened mood. The Egyptians on their side seemed content with their initial gains and waged a comparatively low-keyed war of attrition, advancing their infantry in small leaps at night and mopping up such centers of resistance as had not fallen to the first assault. Had Anwar Sadat accepted the cease fire proposed to him by Henry Kissinger on October 12, the war would have ended in a clearcut, if limited, Egyptian victory. However, apparently in the hope of drawing more blood by enticing the Israelis to renew their counterattacks, the Egyptian President refused. By this time, too, he may have felt obliged to do something in order to help his hard-pressed Syrian allies.

Having spent Friday and Saturday passing their armor over the Canal, the Egyptians attacked on the morning of Sunday, October 14. Their exact objectives are still obscure; in all probability, Sadat did not trust to his army's ability to meet the Israelis in a mobile encounter in the open desert far from the Canal, for such an encounter would require much more speed, coordination, and individual initiative than the Egyptian soldier had hitherto displayed. Even if successful, moreover, advancing deeper into the Sinai would have drawn the army away from the cover provided by the semipermanent antiaircraft missile bases on the west side of the Canal,[30] thus exposing it to annihilation from the sky. Instead of trying to achieve a deep and rapid breakthrough at one or two selected points, therefore, the Egyptian advance was a rather slow, deliberate affair with the pace of the armor tied to that of the infantry and extending along a great part of the front. The results were, perhaps, predictable. The IAF was active all over the battlefield, and highly effective. Using their tanks as antitank guns and exploiting their superior shooting to the full on the ground and in the air, the Israelis inflicted a terrible defeat on the Egyptians, with whole battalions being picked off without a single Israeli tank hit. By midday, with 264 Egyptian tanks burning all over the battlefield,[31] the offensive power of their army was broken for the duration of the war.

Bridging the Canal. Exactly when the Israeli decision to cross the Canal was made we do not know. Such a move had certainly been prepared for insofar as the necessary bridging equipment had been designed and manufactured;[32] according to some sources, the IDF was in a position to put it in effect on the evening of Monday, October 8, when one of its armored battalions had reached the Canal through a gap in the Egyptian lines. Whether deliberately or not, however, its advance was not followed up. Bridging equipment must have been on its way on October 11, and it is probable that the actual crossing was delayed by the Egyptian attack on the 14th. The final decision to move must therefore have been made between the repulse of that attack and noon, October 15.

The man selected to carry out this extremely audacious move was Major-General Ariel Sharon, a flamboyant infantryman and paratrooper who had gained his experience while commanding border raids in the 1950s and as a divisional commander in 1967. Initially, he had luck on his side: his advance brigades found a weakly held gap between the Egyptian Second and Third Armies at the projected crossing point (see Sharon, 1973). Hence, reaching the Canal proved a comparatively easy task; a force attempting to extend the access wedges to the north, however, ran into stiff opposition in the area known as the "Chinese Farm."[33] Here took place one of the toughest battles of the war as the Egyptian Second Army drove down to close the corridor to the Canal and had to be kept off by successive waves of tanks and paratroopers fighting a confused battle with little coordination and less control. In the meantime a single battle brigade was across the water. The battle lasted for two days and the night in between; it was not until October 18 that the corridor was finally widened and secured.

When they reached the Canal, the Israelis had faced the choice of either rolling up the flanks of the two Egyptian Armies to the left and the right or taking the bolder course of crossing the Canal and launching an attack from the rear. The resistance put up by the Second Army to the attempts to extend the corridor northward, as well as the urgent need to reduce losses in the air by knocking out the antiaircraft missiles on the west bank, led to pursual of the second course if, indeed, the first one had been considered at all. During the night of October 15-16, when the advance force had paddled across the Canal, it had met initially with no opposition whatsoever.

On the morning of October 16, the Israelis had begun to pass tanks over the Canal by means of heavy motorized rafts. By this time, the local Egyptian command—though apparently not the central authorities in Cairo, who remained blissfully ignorant of what was taking place[34]—had awakened to the Israeli move, so that the crossing of the tanks, as well as the subsequent bridge-laying, was subjected to heavy artillery fire. On the west bank, meanwhile, an impatient Sharon defied rather cautious orders and sent the few tanks he had available to mount raids all around the initial bridgehead. Meeting at first with practically no opposition, they roamed more or less at will and destroyed a number of antiaircraft missile batteries—the first hole to be punched in Egypt's air defenses since the beginning of the war. Sharon's direct superior, however, a chastened Gonen, ordered him to pull his forces back and refused reinforcements until the battle of the Chinese Farm was over and the Israeli corridor to the east bank of the Canal was secured some 48 hours later. This delay, Sharon subsequently claimed, resulted in Israel throwing away the prospect of a full and complete victory.

By Wednesday, October 17, the Egyptian General Staff had belatedly realized the danger threatening its armies. They started withdrawing some armor from the east side of the Canal, but were hampered in this by the fact that the direction of the main Israeli effort west of it was still unknown.[35] The Israeli Air Force, moreover, had now largely completed its tasks in Syria[36] and, aided by Sharon's forces, who were shooting up the missile sites, gradually recovered its freedom of action. The Egyptian attempt to meet this threat by finally activating their air force resulted in numerous dogfights in which the Egyptians were invariably the losers; the extent of their despair can be gauged from the fact that many of their planes, flying very low, were shot down by Israeli small arms fire. Under the cover of a murderous bombardment, the Israeli advance slowly gathered momentum and became more pronouncedly directed toward the south, toward the encirclement of the Egyptian Third Army. Sharon's force, meanwhile, moved north. By Six Days' War standards, however, the pace of even this flamboyant commander remained slow and cautious to the end. On the west bank of the Canal, there were no elegant victories, only a methodical, brutal pounding by some 300 tanks and perhaps 30,000 other troops. Not daring to send their armor far forward, the Israelis advanced, as they had done on the Syrian front, mainly with mechanized infantry, supported by tanks and artillery. The IDF's superior shooting was exploited to the full with every attempt being made to take up such positions as to compel the Egyptians to attack. Only toward the very end, on October 23rd and 24th, did progress become noticeably faster; but at that time, a United Nations cease-fire had already been proclaimed.

III. THE LESSONS

Surprise aside, Israel's generals won the Six Days War by superior mobility, both tactical and strategic; six years later, her rank and file won the Yom Kippur War—if won it was—by superior shooting. In the first case, a quick and elegant victory was achieved by the swift thrust of a rapier that moved, pierced, outflanked, and cut off; in the second, a bloody but incomplete triumph was obtained by the heavy pounding of a bludgeon that smashed, crushed, and destroyed. At the same time, shock had lost in importance as against firepower; maneuver as against attrition; and quality as against quantity. The result was not merely a different war but a new type of warfare.

This, however, is putting things in a nutshell. In order to discuss the implications of the Yom Kippur War more fully we shall assume, as we did in the introduction to this study, that while "accidental" factors connected with time and place do much to mold the peculiarities of each specific conflict, its place in the more general history of warfare is dictated, broadly, by the nature of the technical means employed. Weapons determine tactics—that is the character of the battlefield; while tactics in their turn determine strategy—that is the character of war. We shall therefore start our discussion by considering weapons, passing on to tactics, and from there to strategy. True, this procedure is not an ideal one. In some cases, the distinction between the three stages may become blurred. Also, since additional "accidental" factors must enter the picture at each successive stage, the discussion will of need become more and more general; imagination must play its part. While a precise description of the next war can hardly be expected, one can at least make an informed guess about some of its outstanding characteristics.

The Weapons

Any discussion of the lessons of the Yom Kippur War in relation to the future development of arms must obviously start with an examination of that centerpiece of the modern battle, the tank. Following the reserves inflicted on the "best tankmen in the world"—as the Israelis were sometimes called—observers writing immediately after the war were inclined to write off the tank as a weapon doomed to disappearance (see Smart, 1973). The Yom Kippur War, and especially the events of October 8, were compared to the battle of Crecy in 1346 A.D.: just as the English longbow overcame the armored knight, it was claimed, so the antitank missile was about to blast the tank off the battlefield and thereby open a new epoch in warfare. While the fundamental thought underlying the comparison may be sound, it is oversimplified even in its own terms: it overlooks the fact that knights in armor did survive on the battlefields of Europe for some 200 years after Crecy—indeed, that they did so for a period considerably longer than that of the longbow itself.

The tank was invented some sixty years ago specifically to cope with that fundamental problem, namely survival on a modern fire-swept battlefield that had already become too hot for any other arm (see Fuller, 1945: 139 ff.). Alone among the weapon systems of the time, it could withstand, and not merely avoid, hostile fire; hence tanks were able to reintroduce shock action into warfare, an advantage that proved sufficiently great for them to play a crucial role in the last years of World War I. The early tanks were slow, cumbrous engines, but when technological progress enabled their hitting and receiving power to be combined with mobility, unheard-of possibilities resulted. Antitank weapons were invented almost immediately, but they lagged behind the tank in mobility and protection; furthermore, since their ability to penetrate armor depended on high velocity projectiles and a heavy punch—most easily built into a heavy vehicle—the tank held an advantage that made it into its own most dangerous enemy. It was not until the invention, in the last years of World War II, of an armor-piercing warhead not dependent on a heavy punch—the hollow charge—that antitank weapons could be made sufficiently light to be used by infantrymen; and even then it took another quarter of a century to perfect carrying and aiming devices so as to make their use anything but suicidal.[37] The result was that, while the tank's mobility and striking power were not seriously put in question by the Yom Kippur War,[38] its ability to protect itself—the very quality for which it was originally designed—was put in doubt by Ahmed Ismail's infantrymen.

The Future of Armor. Fundamentally, there are two ways to solve this problem. First, armor may be increased; second, low-density armor may be used. The difficulty, however, is that the types of armor—either spaced or consisting of a low density plastic coat—that will afford protection against the hollow charge will not do the same for conventional armor-piercing missiles. This is a baffling dilemma that has not so far been resolved. Whatever the solution ultimately adopted, the addition of more armor can hardly be achieved without some loss of mobility; and even if this loss can be compensated for by stronger engines, strategic mobility will certainly be diminished. For reasons to be discussed later, however, precisely such mobility is likely to be of crucial importance in the future. Thus, the problem remains.

More attractive at first sight is an approach that would aim at enabling the tank to avoid, instead of withstand, the threat presented by hostile firepower. To this purpose, tanks must either be made smaller—so as to present more difficult targets—or sufficiently mobile to enable them to take evasive action and use cover. The first approach has been adopted by the Swedes and led to the development of the Strv-103 turretless tanks; the second lies behind the German Leopard and the French AMX-30. Both have their drawbacks. Some of the advantages of giving up the turret—notably smaller size and a reduced crew—are likely to be lost again by the need to have secondary armament, a need that, given the new power of the infantry as well as the aircraft threat, will certainly prove even more important in the future. Other things equal, lighter vehicles are inherently less capable of delivering a heavy punch. Thus, the baby is in danger of being thrown out with the water.

This brings us to the armament of future tanks.[39] Here, the war has highlighted the issue of guns versus guided missiles. The greatest advantages of the missiles are their accuracy at long range and, above all, their ability to give great striking power to a comparatively light vehicle. Their drawbacks are equally obvious; except as a means of engaging the most difficult targets, missiles are impossibly expensive. Their bulk means that only a few can be carried, while the need of present-generation equipment to be optically guided to its target prevents the tank from taking cover for a few seconds after firing. Given these difficulties, together with the gun's ability to fire a variety of different types of ammunition, it seems that tank-guns are not on their way to the scrap-yard. The ultimate solution, if any, is difficult to envisage at this date. It has been suggested that fin-stabilized ammunition may increase the proportion of a shell's length to its diameter and thus give better armor-piercing qualities, making possible the first reduction of gun calibers since the invention of the tank. Alternatively, one may envisage a dual purpose system on the lines of the American Shillalegh, capable of firing both missiles for long-range antitank work and ballistic ammunition for most other purposes. In both cases, smaller, lighter, more maneuverable vehicles could result.

One aspect of tank armament that will certainly have to undergo improvement is that of range-finding and directing systems. The excellent Israeli shooting that did so much to shape the Yom Kippur War was due, to a large extent, to the equipment of Israeli tanks with superior range-finding equipment. Still, as compared to the electronic marvels incorporated in modern aircraft, tanks are rather primitive in this respect—a fact that worked in favor of the IDF by enabling it to bring its superior quality to bear. As to the future, the greatest promise seems to lie in systems integrating lasers and computers such as the Belgian-made COBELDA; such systems should be able not merely to find the range but also to compensate for wind, barrel wear, and turret traverse. The result will be to make tanks simpler to operate; on the other hand, maintenance problems are going to be compounded. Cost will also rise.

The Future of Artillery. If the tank is a weapon that, given the terrain, both sides in the Middle East have always made extensive use of, artillery by contrast has been strongly emphasized by the Arabs while suffering from comparative neglect in Israel. This neglect is readily understandable from Israel's traditional reliance on mobile, quick-moving warfare; the weight and bulk associated with artillery—from the catapult onward—have always tended to make it turn out to best advantage under conditions of more or less static warfare. Historically, guns first became really important during the siege-warfare of the fifteenth century, but 400 years of development had to pass until they could be made sufficiently mobile to enable them, in Napoleon's words, to "decide the fate of nations." Even then, however, they were soon outstripped by the more rapid evolution of small arms whose fire dominated the battlefields from the middle of the nineteenth century onward. It was only when this fire ended up by virtually paralyzing all tactical movement that artillery really came into its own; under the siege-like conditions of World War I it became the dominant, all-powerful arm to which all others were mere appendages. Since then, however, the advent of armor has not only led to the tanks taking over some of the functions traditionally associated with artillery but also eroded the importance of artillery by restoring tactical mobility. It is no accident, therefore, that artillery figures least in those military doctrines putting the greatest emphasis on speed and mobility, namely the German Blitzkrieg technique and, to some extent, present-day Soviet doctrine that has led to conventional guns being largely replaced by short- and medium-range ballistic missiles for use against the rear, rather than the front, of the opposing forces.

Insofar as the Yom Kippur War has shown the limits of armored mobility, however, and also because it witnessed a significant reverse inflicted on the fighter bomber, artillery is very likely to rise in importance in the near future. While this much seems certain, the war has done little to answer the question of which kind of artillery is preferable. Should guns be mounted on wheels and drawn by motor vehicles, as they are on Soviet field models? Or should they be mounted on tracks and made fully independent, as American ones are? No definite answer can be given. In the past, the advantages of the first approach—simplicity and relative cheapness, making possible mass use—have been contrasted with those of the second, the ability of the guns to accompany the tanks on their tactical missions. The Yom Kippur War has modified these considerations insofar as it gave reason to think that tactical movement on the battlefields of the future will become slower, rather than faster; on the other hand, there stand the benefits the Israelis derived from their guns' ability to rapidly change their positions and thus escape the counterbattery fire of the overwhelmingly numerous Arab batteries. While this kind of "jumping" from cover to cover will presumably become more important in the future—especially if, as has been suggested, artillery is going to be equipped with laser-based target-designation systems—it is also imperative to balance tactical against strategic mobility. Exactly how all these conflicting demands are going to be met I cannot presume to say. Be this as it may, there can be little doubt but that the star of the artillery is on the ascendant and that it is about to resume a more important role than has been the case at any time since the end of World War I.

The Armored Personnel Carrier. The next weapon with which we have to deal is the Armored Personnel Carrier (APC). Originally, the tank itself was nothing but an APC; its task was to get men and weapons across no-man's land and into enemy lines, not to engage others of its own kind. "The tank of today carries forward the rifleman of the future" (Fuller, 1936b: 129); expected to help overcome field fortifications, the early tanks were armed, logically enough, with machine guns to deal with enemy infantry. Only at a later date did it become clear that the tank was its own worst enemy; this, together with the tendency to make tanks operate independently ahead of the rest of the army, led to an overspecialization not unlike that of the medieval knight and to a gradual loss of the tank's ability to defend itself against well-armed and determined infantry. The tank's overspecialization made it necessary for it to be closely supported by infantry, which could be done only if infantry were provided with vehicles possessing cross-country capability comparable to that of the tanks themselves; hence the half-tracks used by many armies in World War II. The infantry, however, had to dismount in order to go into action and it was at this point that they became vulnerable to artillery; it was only the IDF's weakness in this arm,[40] combined with the Arabs' indifference to casualties, that allowed the Egyptians in particular to operate as they did. Rather than pointing to any increase in the relative importance of foot soldiers, therefore, the Yom Kippur War demonstrates the need to put the infantry behind some kind of armor plate.

To do this, a number of different vehicles have been developed. On one hand there are the American and British "tin box" APCs built to bring troops to the battlefield; on the other, the German (Marder) and Soviet BMP Infantry Fighting Vehicles (IFV) are designed to participate in the action itself. While it would clearly be impossible to point to any one method as correct under all circumstances there can be no doubt but that the Yom Kippur War proved, if proof were needed, the advantages of fighting mounted; this, even in the case of vehicles that, like the American M-113, were not primarily designed for this task. In any case, even an APC not designed for mounted action should have weapons for close support; the day of the unarmed battlefield "taxi" is definitely over.

Since action against enemy infantry and close support must be the IFV's first task, it should be mounted with machine guns, grenade launchers and possibly flame throwers. At the same time, it must have some kind of fighting chance against enemy tanks—and to this purpose a recoilless rifle shooting HEAT shells would be suitable. To hit targets farther away, antitank missiles could also be carried, though their number must necessarily be strictly limited. The present-day vehicle that comes closest to fulfilling these demands is the Soviet-built BMP-76, probably the best of its kind in the world (though like other Russian AFVs it is impossibly cramped). If the Yom Kippur War has proved anything, it is the need for the West to have a similar vehicle, and soon.

As IFVs are furnished with increasingly powerful armament, they will presumably tend to grow heavier. As tanks increase their secondary armament, and also come to rely on movement rather than armor for protection, they will tend to resemble IFVs. The ultimate result, though this is still some way off, may very well be a fusion of the two types of weapons—a process not unlike that which, following the invention of the bayonet in the late seventeenth century, enabled the individual foot-soldier to use both shock and fire and thus eliminated the need for two separate categories of troops armed with pike and musket respectively. The form of such a vehicle, which would enormously facilitate the problems of tactical coordination, can scarcely be imagined at present. It will, presumably, be heavier than present day IFVs, possess very high maneuverability combined with a low silhouette, and be armed with a very high velocity gun of relatively small caliber. Thus it will be able to carry a considerable quantity of ammunition and, when applied to a comparatively light vehicle designed principally to fight against large numbers of its own kind, would be preferable to the bulk associated with guided missiles.

The Antitank Missile. This, in turn, brings us to the future of the antitank missile, which surely deserves to stand out as the symbol of the Yom Kippur War. Though highly effective and simple to operate, these missiles are not without their defects. Most of them, including the Sagger itself, must be "gathered" on target, a process that takes several seconds and makes them useless at short range. All have to be guided, whether manually or optically, to their targets, thus exposing their operators to fire. At best, only one missile and targeting device can be carried by each soldier—and in most cases two or three are needed to fire just one "round." All these factors tend to make the missile a rather wasteful weapon, liable to be extremely expensive in numbers —the Syrians and Egyptians probably fired dozens of missiles for every tank put out of action—and in human casualties. Theoretically, it should perhaps be possible to overcome these difficulties by building missiles capable of independently identifying and following their targets (as several air-to-air and air-to-surface missiles already do) but the cost of using such devices against anything but the most important targets would be prohibitive. Perhaps the best guess for the near future would be a system such as the British Swingfire, which, by allowing the operator to control the missile while staying under cover as much as 50 meters away, increases his safety.

As things stand at present, operating antitank missiles depends on stealth; consequently, they are eminently suited for the defense but much less so for the attack. This is likely to remain so for some time to come; though the missiles can readily be mounted atop vehicles, they will, as we have seen, complement rather than replace the gun of the AFV (Armored Fighting Vehicle) of the future. There is, however, another engine for which these missiles seem ideally suitable, namely the attack helicopter; equipped with, for example, American TOW missiles, the attack helicopter could develop into a real "tank killer." In the Yom Kippur War, neither side possessed this weapon; both, however, are likely to do so in the future.[41] Exactly what their effect will be remains to be seen. Experience in Vietnam and maneuvers conducted by NATO have clearly shown the superiority of helicopters over tanks, but if the war has shown anything at all it is that tanks are very unlikely indeed to be on their own in any future conflict. Considering the newly-found effectiveness of antiaircraft defenses, particularly that of the light shoulder-fired missiles such as the SAM-7, whose warheads are too small to seriously damage conventional planes but highly dangerous against helicopters, it is more than doubtful that helicopters could survive on a modern battlefield. Certainly, they will have to fly very low—if only to avoid hostile fighter aircraft—and to make extensive use of natural obstacles and cover; even so, however, their vulnerability remains a problem. Rather than playing a great role on the battlefield, therefore, helicopters are likely to continue to be used on its edge, and particularly against such tanks as may have succeeded in penetrating the front and getting behind it. Operating in this role they may well present a new and deadly threat to the tank.

The Air Defenses. Passing on to the air force, it is almost unnecessary to dwell on the magnitude of the role played by antiaircraft defenses in the Yom Kippur War. Whereas, in 1967, after the first air strike, everything Arab caught moving was mercilessly destroyed; and whereas, before October 6, 1973, it was widely believed that no conventional operation—let alone a large-scale offensive over open terrain—could succeed in the face of enemy air superiority; these beliefs were shattered during the very first hours of the Yom Kippur War. True, the Arab success was strictly limited and won at tremendous cost; the Egyptians are said to have employed three times as many men in their antiaircraft defenses as in their air force (75,000 to 23,000). Israeli losses, it should be remembered, dropped sharply after the first three days of the war,[42] and "smart" bombs now being introduced may go some, though hardly all, of the way toward solving the problem.[43] Whatever the ultimate outcome of the struggle of plane against missile, it would be no exaggeration to say that the Yom Kippur War has fundamentally altered the relationship between them. Both will, no doubt, continue to improve: ECM (Electronic Counter Measures) and EECM (Electronic Counter-Counter Measures) will be developed at an ever increasing rate (see International Defense Review, 1973: 700), and a growing proportion of military budgets will go to the electronics companies. At one point or another, however, air forces are bound to discover that their electronic "tail" is so large compared to the fighting "teeth" as to make the whole exercise unprofitable.

Though the end of the manned fighter bomber is still nowhere near, greater thought will certainly have to be devoted in the future to alternative ways of delivering warheads. To this end, two weapons clearly suggest themselves. The first is the unmanned "drone," which the IDF is already adopting; it is useful both for work against air defenses and for reconnaissance. Second, the difficulties encountered by aircraft will again raise the question of replacing them by short- and medium-range surface-to-surface missiles. Hitherto the latter have usually been considered too wasteful and too inaccurate for tactical missions unless equipped with nuclear warheads; but the check imposed on the fighter bomber in the Yom Kippur War as well as much improved accuracies have led to a rethinking of this issue. The result is likely to be, not the disappearance of manned aircraft, but their integration with other weapons in a closely-knit team affording mutual support.

To come back to the air defenses themselves, their newly-found effectiveness is certainly one of the most important lessons to emerge from the war. Particular mention should be made of the SAM-6 guided missile and the radar-guided, four-barrelled ZSU-23 cannon, which together give necessary good cover at all altitudes up to 50,000 feet. As compared to the earlier SAM-2 and SAM-3, the greatest advantages of both are their mobility and the ease with which they can be deployed, factors that must be of crucial importance if antiaircraft defenses are ever to become flexible enough, not merely to cover set-piece battles over a limited area but for use in strategically mobile campaigns. At present, the greatest drawback of the missile is undoubtedly the handicap it imposes, not merely on the enemy but on one's own air force as well. The Syrians are reported to have shot down no less than twenty Iraqi planes in the course of a single day, and the need to keep the skies clear for the missiles was undoubtedly one of the principal reasons behind the relative inactivity of the Egyptian Air Force. Consequently, it is imperative to solve the problem of IFF (Identification Friend-Foe) if the missiles are to be employed in theaters of war not dominated, as was the case in both Vietnam and the Middle East, by the planes of one side.

In summarizing this section, the most important conclusion to emerge is that the days of any so-called "king of the battlefield" and "master weapon," both on the ground and in the air, are definitely over. No single arm, much less any individual technical instrument, is alone capable of winning or even dominating a modern war. If it is historically true that a "master weapon"—be it the Macedonian phalanx or the medieval knight—tends to respond to the challenges put in its way by developing to the point of overspecialization until a breaking point is reached (Wintringham, 1943: 30-31), this breaking point seems to be on the horizon for both tank and fighter bomber in the sense that they cannot now be considered "weapons of the future." Contrary to what was written immediately after the war, neither of them stands in any imminent danger of disappearing from the battlefield; both, however, have already lost a good deal of their former dominance and their continued survival must depend above all on close integration with other arms. Taking a more general view, the Yom Kippur War may perhaps be seen in the context of a long-term shift away from large and expensive weapons-systems, toward smaller, cheaper ones relying less on individual action than on mass; if this interpretation is correct, a far-reaching change in the nature of warfare may well be in the making.

Tactics, or the Character of Battle

Weapon development is broadly dictated by technological possibilities ("the state of the art") and is therefore likely to run along more or less parallel lines in the most advanced countries; not so tactics, which must of necessity display a much greater variety. The nature of the terrain; the task at hand; the intentions and capabilities of the enemy; all these are "accidental" factors that will do much to determine the tactics employed at any given time and place. For this reason, the following survey must remain general and limit itself to those aspects of tactics that are more or less applicable everywhere in large-scale conventional war because they are dictated by the characteristics of modern arms; returning to our original definition of tactics as a combination of methods for striking, moving, and protecting, the problem is whether the Yom Kippur War has witnessed a shift in the dominant combinations utilized and, if so, what the implications of this shift are likely to be.

Any discussion of tactics must start with the most important lesson of the war, namely the inability of armor to withstand, not merely the firepower delivered by tanks or from the air, but that of small, relatively inexpensive, easy-to-operate infantry weapons capable of being produced and used on a huge scale. Assuming that armor is not about to regain its protective power—a development that, for reasons outlined in the previous section, does not appear likely—other ways of affording protection will have to be found; these, in turn, will necessarily affect the methods used for striking and moving. In our attempts to understand the implications of these changes we are fortunate in that such a process is not unique in history; a similar one took place in the fifteenth and sixteenth centuries. It is there, accordingly, that we should look for our guidelines.

The defeat of the armored knight, first by the English longbow and then by early firearms, was naturally followed by a decline in the importance of cavalry relative to that of the infantry. Initially, the heavy cavalry tended to become even heavier, but this was compensated for by the appearance of a new class of light cavalry, namely the Venetian *sardiots,* the Spanish *ginetores,* and the English demi-lances. Artillery, which initially had much more to say in siege operations than on the battlefield proper, gradually increased in importance as the guns were made more mobile. Given all these new arms, coordination among them —practically nonexistent in a period when heavy cavalry could decide battles on its own—became the crucial factor on which turned victory and defeat. Skirmishing and fire-action now opened every battle and frequently brought it to a decision. The coup de grace was still normally delivered by the heavy cavalry which, kept out of the way in the first stages of the clash, would thunder into the fray at the decisive moment. Pursuit and exploitation were left to the light horse since the heavy cavalry was too precious to be risked. As cover and field fortifications gained in importance, battlefields tended to grow and fronts to spread out. Tactical movement generally tended to become slower and more cautious, a process that was not reversed until the days of Cromwell and Gustavus Adolphus.[44]

Assuming that a similar shift away from armor is now taking place, which of these developments can be regarded as relevant to our own day? Some of them, notably the division of the "cavalry" into heavy and light branches—tanks and IFVs—are materializing before our eyes; the ultimate outcome of this particular trend, indeed, may yet be a compromise (à la Marlborough). Similarly, the relationship between infantry and "cavalry" is changing. Since foot-soldiers armed with guided missiles will be expecting the advancing tanks behind every bush and rise in the ground, tanks will either have to become less specialized or to be reserved for special circumstances. Though the tanks' secondary armament is likely to become vastly more important—in a way rather similar to that which saw sixteenth century cavalry adopting the pistol in addition to the lance—this will hardly permit them anything like their old freedom of movement. Casting about slowly and cautiously, tanks will have to keep their distance from well-armed infantry[45] and consequently forfeit their ability to use shock action. At best, this will be possible only against an enemy already more than half defeated by other means. Such armored charges as we are likely to witness in the future will come at the end, rather than the beginning, of the battle.

Tank-to-tank warfare, too, is undergoing a change. While it is true that armor has never afforded sufficient protection against point-blank hits, improved directing and range-finding equipment will mean that tanks will be unable to face each other in the open. Consequently, much greater use than hitherto must be made of prepared positions, ramparts, and cover. Advances and retreats will take place in short, breathless rushes. Tanks will shoot with their hulls down, withdraw from sight after one or two shots, and rapidly change their positions. Artillery cover will be essential for safety at all times. Dispersion and extreme tactical flexibility must be the order of the day; under such conditions, centralized control will be difficult and "battles" may tend to degenerate into a series of individual actions. Since armor no longer affords anything like sufficient protection against direct hits, everything will come to depend on the ability to fire first, quickly, and accurately. This will place a premium on "stalking warfare," pouncing and retreating, as waged by the IDF while defending the Golan Heights. What is likely to happen to tanks advancing in close order, and without making use of cover, was amply demonstrated by the casualties inflicted on the Syrians in the Golan Heights, the Israelis in their counterattack of October 8, and, above all, by the fate meted out to the Egyptians in their disastrous advance of October 14.

In any case, tanks are highly unlikely to be on their own in any future conflict. A number of spectacular victories notwithstanding, the attempt to turn a machine originally invented for siege operations into mechanized cavalry has failed (see Orgill, 1970: 248-254). The day of armored divisions operating separately from, and often far ahead of, their own armies is over for good. Nor will tanks necessarily form the first echelon of the tactical advance. Rather, like the heavy cavalry of the fifteenth and sixteenth centuries, it will have to form the linchpin of a closely integrated battle team, incorporating in addition the artillery, as well as antitank weapons, IFVs, and, in special cases, infantry on foot. Advances will probably be spearheaded by AFVs and supported by tanks rather than vice versa. In both defense and attack, success will depend on the ability to use each of the different kinds of troops for their proper function and at the proper moment. To this purpose, organizational changes must take place. Traditional "arms" such as the infantry or artillery are about to become obsolete as all save a relative handful of specialist troops and reserves are swallowed up in a more or less homogeneous army. Exactly how such an army should be organized to ensure maximum flexibility is very hard to say. Possibly, it should consist entirely of armored and mechanized divisions differing from each other mainly in the proportion of tanks to AFVS.[46] Also, intermediate units such as regiment and brigade will have to go; a division will consist of so many battalions of different types plus a number of independent headquarters ready to take command over any combination of them in accordance with tactical requirements. In this respect the American ROAD division may well point the way to the future.

The increased vulnerability of armor will, as already noted, make cover vastly more important. Using the terrain necessarily entails dispersion and, since armies are hardly likely to become smaller, an enlarged battlefield. One can also guess that this battlefield will be much emptier than has been the case during the last 50 years or so. There will be comparatively little to see. No compact tank formations will drive against hostile fronts or engage in maneuvering against each other. No masses of vehicles will move about in clouds of dust, protected by aircraft overhead, instead, there will be an emptiness that will stand out even more because of the increased ranges made possible by new direction-finding equipment. One will see a flash here, followed by a column of smoke there; a long barrel suddenly appearing against the skyline and immediately vanishing again; the blazing trails left by guided missiles followed, presumably, by the crash of artillery shooting at the infantrymen; slow, painful advances from one natural obstacle to the next; a great many intricately-linked minefields, antitank ditches, and other artificial obstacles designed not so much to stop movement as to channel it into preselected "killing grounds"; here and there, possibly, the rapid appearance and immediate disappearance of a comparatively light vehicle designed to draw fire; and helicopters lurking at some distance, ready to pounce on anything that still threatens to engage on larger tactical movements. Such, presumably, will be the appearance of the battlefield of the future.

Given the increasing vulnerability of planes to air defenses, cooperation between air and ground forces will become much closer than was hitherto the case. If the air force has traditionally been used to clear the way for the ground forces, the reverse may now become equally frequent. Long-range artillery and surface-to-surface missiles are very likely to be used against air defenses: the former for action against the lighter and more mobile types, the latter against fixed installations that, due to their size and the extreme delicacy of the instruments involved, present tempting targets. Were air force not needed to retain not merely tactical but strategic flexibility—that is, the ability to switch rapidly from one theater of war to another—there would certainly be a case in favor of abolishing it altogether as a separate arm and for finding some way to incorporate its various components into the homogeneous army mentioned above. As it is, however, no such development seems likely to take place in the near future. The problem of air-ground cooperation will have to be solved by the allocation of more forward observers and liaison officers, better instruction of the ground troops in the possibilities and limitations of air power,[47] and improved channels of communication between the front and the air bases behind it. Dominating everything, however, will be the imperative need for aircraft to look after their own safety first. Even at best, their tactical environment is likely to be more lethal than ever before. Certainly, antiaircraft defenses have a long way to go if planes are ever going to disappear from the battlefield. However, enough has already been achieved to turn them into the partners, rather than masters, of the ground forces.

As usually happens in periods when firepower is on the ascendance, it is the tactical defense that stands to gain most. If the longbow enabled the English to win a whole series of defensive battles in the fourteenth and fifteenth centuries; if, in the middle of the nineteenth century, the development of small-arm firepower caused frontal attacks delivered against prepared enemies to fail "on every occasion" from 1861 onward (Fuller, 1962: 104); so, in our own day, the advent of the antitank missile has vastly increased the possibilities of the defense. If, at the end of World War II, a three-to-one superiority in overall numbers and a five-to-one superiority along the principal axis of advance was needed in order to successfully attack an enemy who was neither unprepared nor hopelessly inferior in quality (Hart, 1960: 104-109), the Yom Kippur War has shown that this disparity is likely to grow still further in the future.

Exactly how the tactical defense must be conducted in each

case will, of course, depend on circumstances. Contrary to what is usually believed, however, the Yom Kippur War has not proved the worthlessness of fixed defenses. Rather, it has shown the speed with which such defenses may be improvised—within 36 hours after the initial crossings the Egyptian lines had been made sufficiently strong to withstand all Israeli counterattacks. True, the vaunted Bar Lev Line fell with unexpected ease; this, however, may have been due more to the fact that only half of the strongholds were manned with half the necessary troops than to any inherent weakness of the static defense. On the Golan Heights, all but one of the eleven Israeli strongholds held out to the end and, though isolated and under heavy attack, served a useful purpose in canalizing the Syrian advance. If, as history shows, the defense tends to gain most from the advent of firepower, this is largely due to the greater ease with which a man or machine can shoot a missile while standing still than a man or machine that does so on the move and must consequently present a larger target while unable to use cover. A mobile defense may be ideal—indeed, it may well present the only possible defense—under conditions of highly mobile warfare based on shock and rapid maneuver such as obtained in the early years of World War II; when firepower dominates the battlefield, however, reliance on mobile warfare may well cause the defender to forfeit most of his advantages. Given the power of modern artillery it may be argued that fixed positions should rely on depth and dispersion rather than on their own strength for protection, with a greater emphasis on field fortifications as against permanent structures. Be this as it may, it is a historical fact that every growth in the importance of firepower has been accompanied by an increment in the role of fixed positions, be it the stakes and ditches of the fourteenth century or the wooden breastworks of the nineteenth. There is every reason to believe that the present cycle will prove no exception.

How, given the new power of the tactical defense, offensive operations are to be conducted is mainly a strategic problem that will be discussed in the next section. Here, it is important to point out once more the greater role artillery will play in the tactical offensive. Since the tank—the main offensive weapon of the last 50 years—cannot easily overcome or brush aside a well-constructed modern defense, it will be necessary to blast through. Only artillery, with its ability to deliver accurate and, above all, sustained fire can fulfill this need. Again, historical precedents readily suggest themselves. A couple of culverins, placed on a flank, finally enabled the French to defeat the English defensive array at Formigny in 1452. From the middle of the nineteenth century onward, artillery tended to become the main offensive arm, and it was the superiority of their breech-loading steel guns—rather than any reliance on small arms fire, in which they were actually inferior—that enabled the Prussians to win the war of 1870-1871 (Howard, 1961: 7). If, since the monstrous barrages of 1916-1917, artillery preparation has on the whole tended to become shorter, with tactical aircraft taking over part of the job; if the guns have been used to support, rather than lead, the advance; this tendency may well be reversed in the future.

Meanwhile, the advantages of the defense have been indisputably demonstrated by the Yom Kippur War. Consequently, there is reason to think that battles—though not necessarily campaigns—will become harder to decide in the years to come, and will display a growing tendency to degenerate into slugging matches going on interminably until one or the other side gives way because of sheer exhaustion. Under such conditions, ammunition expenditure is likely to rise enormously as will losses in men and materiel. Fire as opposed to shock action; cover against free movement; slaughter as against maneuver; these, presumably, will characterize the tactics of the near future.

Strategy, or the Character of War

In the first book of *On War,* Clausewitz (1962: 100, 107) writes that it is easier to construct a theory for tactics than for strategy. To his mind, this reflects the fact that the clash of weapons—the domain of tactics—produces mainly material results, whereas the higher one ascends on the scale of war, the more numerous and important moral factors become—factors that are much less amenable to incorporation in any theoretical model. At the highest level these factors become so complex as to call for genius; that is, precisely the most "accidental" among those constituents of war whose elimination is essential if history is to be capable of offering any lessons at all. Insofar as tactics are largely dictated by the qualities of the weapons available, it may be permissible to speak of the way battles were fought in this or that period; it is doubtful, however, whether the same can be said of strategy. Strategy is frequently held to be eternally unchanging, and consequently many attempts have been made to reduce it to a series of principles presumably valid for all time.[48] However, if it were true that strategy is eternal—that the fundamentals of war, in Schlieffen's words, have not changed since Cannae—then the question of whether and how any specific historical event affected strategy would be meaningless, and the whole of military science would not amount to more than a few rather banal pages. This, however, is an unwarranted conclusion. Strategy, I shall try to show, *is* affected by tactical changes. Rather than explain the Yom Kippur War in terms of the decisions of Ahmed Ismail and Mustafa Tlas, important as their decisions undoubtedly were, an attempt should be made to see what deeper forces were at work, and how these forces can be expected to operate in the future.

Possibly the strategic issue to be most immediately affected by the tactical changes listed in the previous section is the question of annihilation versus attrition. Putting things in a nutshell, annihilation aims at defeating one's enemy in a single decisive battle, while attrition aims at wearing him down by the gradual application of pressure without any obvious turning point.[49] Though it would be patently absurd to dogmatize on a matter subject to so many complex considerations, there can be little doubt but that, on the whole, any increase in the importance of firepower and consequent strengthening of the defense favors the attrition as against the annihilation. Few if any decisive battles have ever been won by means of the tactical defense alone; even at Crecy, that supreme example of an army's stupidity in hurling itself against prepared defenses, the coup de grace was delivered by the English men at arms (see Lot, 1946: 343). Assuming that modern armies, unlike the medieval French, will not require a Poitiers and an Agincourt in order to appreciate the lessons of the Yom Kippur War, the check inflicted on the main offensive weapons—tank and aircraft—may well lead to prolonged wars of attrition that neither side will be able to push through to a decision. Here, again, historical precedents are readily available. The American Civil War, the Russo-Japanese War, and World War I were all characterized by the dominance of firepower and the superiority of the tactical defense. Despite the enormous size of the battles that took place in each, there is no instance of the army of any side being annihilated, and all these conflicts were finally decided by sheer exhaustion.

This, however, is not true of the other major wars of the same era, namely the Austro-Prussian and Franco-Prussian Wars of 1866 and 1870, which in this respect may point the way to the future. Though the superiority of the defense was equally evident in these two wars—the Todtenritte of the French at Gravelotte and of von Bredow's hussars at Mars la Tour have become famous—both were decided by great battles of annihilation at Königgrätz, Metz, and Sedan. The reason for this was that, alone in the world, the Prussian army under Helmut von Moltke not only realized the superiority of the defense (Howard, 1961: 7) but also consciously set about to produce a solution that seems equally relevant to the problems of our own day. Moltke's doctrine consisted essentially of two very simple propositions. The first of these was the realization that the advantages of the tactical defense can be offset by strategic maneuver; the second was that the aim of such maneuver should be to seize positions that would compel the enemy to take the tactical initiative (Howard, 1961: 7). The resulting strategy successfully compensated for the weakness of the tactical defense by working on external, rather than internal, lines and aimed at concentrating the German armies on, instead of before, the battlefield. This, at the time, was an innovation and led to a dispute over the question of which of the two kinds of strategy—Napoleon's, working on internal lines, or Moltke's, moving along external ones—was inherently superior.[50]

Looking back at this argument, one suspects that it was based on a fundamental misunderstanding. The superiority of this or that form of strategy is not fixed for all time but is at least partly dependent on changing tactical conditions. Again, it would be absurd to dogmatize; however, a very rough relationship can be worked out. Since operations on internal lines depend on an army's ability to rapidly dispose of one opponent after the other, such a strategy requires that the offense be stronger than the defense, or at least that the habitual disparity between them should not be too great. When such conditions do not obtain, however, the primacy of the defense will, on the whole, favor operations on external lines. This fact can be readily illustrated from the history of the past century and a half, which, on the whole, was a period characterized by the ever-increasing dominance of firepower as opposed to shock. Napoleon's strategy of internal lines was nowhere more successful than in his early Italian campaigns; by the time of Leipzig, however, conditions had already changed sufficiently for the Allies to defeat him by operating on external lines. A year later, despite a dazzling display of some of the most brilliant generalship ever, Napoleon's operations on internal lines did not save him from destruction. From that time onward every major conflict was won by the side operating on external lines, namely 1861-1865, 1866, 1870-1871, 1904-1905, and 1914-1918. The early years of World War II, by reintroducing shock action and thereby increasing the power of the offensive, momentarily reversed the trend; however, it soon reasserted itself.

If the above analysis is correct, the indecisive results of the Yom Kippur War may have been partly due to the fact that, under the new conditions, Israel's—or anybody else's—internal lines no longer confer as great an advantage as they did only a short time ago. The war has shown that it is no longer possible to count on rapidly defeating one opponent before turning to face the other; conversely, the side operating on external lines has more time for mutual support. Given the immense strength of the tactical defense as demonstrated during the war, strategic maneuver on external lines may well be the only possible solution facing the offense if the wars of the future are to be fought to decisions and not merely to end in murderous stalemates. To carry out such maneuvering great mobility is required; and the importance of strategic mobility is definitely one of the principal lessons to emerge from the Yom Kippur War. Whether and by what means such mobility can be achieved we are unable to discuss here; and while Israel is fortunate in that distances between it and its enemies' centers of power are not too large, it is worth pointing out that the "transport revolution" notwithstanding, the pace of strategic movement has grown little over the past two centuries. In this respect, if in no other, a Washington, a Napoleon, and a Sherman were able to perform just as well as did George Patton—not exactly a slow-moving commander—when he was "touring France with an army" in 1944.[51] Clearly, the enormous quantity of supplies consumed by modern armies has tended to neutralize any gains made by motorization; Napoleon's armies could, when pressed, carry all the subsistence they needed for six to eight days on the soldiers' backs, but no such sustained independence from base is conceivable at a time when food forms only a small fraction of total requirements (see Brown, 1963: 208-212). These requirements tend to grow with mechanization; consequently, there has been a tendency, even in the case of fully motorized armies, for strategic movement—even when unopposed—to grind to a halt after 200-300 miles.[52] Experience in World War II and Korea showed that campaigns must be decided before this limit is reached; where this cannot be done stalemate is likely to ensue.

Given the above considerations, one may doubt whether the pace and range of strategic mobility stand any real prospect of being greatly increased in the near future; the Yom Kippur War, however, has drawn attention to another relevant factor. The air force, which since the Spanish Civil War has enabled the side that dominated the sky to destroy much of the movement that took place on the battlefield, has now lost part of its mastery. The full effect of this development on strategic mobility did not come to light during the Yom Kippur War because most of the air defenses of both sides—the SAM-2, SAM-3, and Hawk antiaircraft missiles —were permanently based or at best only semimobile;[53] however, modern systems now becoming operational are fully capable of keeping up with the ground forces and may well make their movements considerably more secure than has been the case for a long time.[54]

Assuming that strategic movement will, in this sense, become easier during the years to come, several changes are likely to take place. First to be affected will be the question of which form of defense—forward or rear—is to be preferred. In the past, there have been many occasions when the domination of the air by one side forced the other to take up a forward defense against his better judgment.[55] This whole issue will require re-examination in the light of the check inflicted on the fighter bomber in the Yom Kippur War, and the conclusion may well be that the reserves employed on a mobile "rear" defense now stand a greater chance of reaching the threatened sector of the front in time than was formerly the case. A conclusion similarly favorable to the defense emerges when one considers that, in the past, the ability of armored and mechanized forces to launch pencil-like thrusts deep into the enemy's rear depended above all on the air force's ability to isolate the battlefield and keep off counterattacks (see Miksche, 1944: 77). If no such conditions obtain, Guderian-like advances carried out "regardless of flanks" (Guderian, 1967: 69)[56] will be exceedingly dangerous, as the Israelis discovered when they put themselves between the Egyptian Second and Third Armies. Penetration into the rear with open flanks is possible only when no effective counterattacks are to be expected, and when this cannot be guaranteed a return to a Schlieffen- or Eisenhower-style battalion carré advancing shoulder to shoulder on a broad front may well become necessary.

Given the above considerations, the future of conventional warfare may perhaps be best envisaged in terms of mechanized armies acting like huge revolving doors, each trying to outflank the other without being outflanked itself. Aware of the power of the defense to bring tactical maneuvering to a halt, commanders will do everything possible to make such maneuvering unnecessary by concentrating on strategic movement along external lines. Move around the enemy, open new fronts; these must be the watchwords of the strategist of the future. As an additional way of getting into the enemy's rear, "vertical envelopment" may be used, as was done on a smallish scale during the Yom Kippur War; however, the difficulty of landing and maintaining a large force behind the enemy lines is such that, except for very exceptional cases, the use of airborne troops is likely to remain tactical rather than strategic for some time to come.[57] While the ability of aircraft to deliver large quantities of supplies over large distances has been demonstrated as never before by the airlifts mounted by both superpowers during the war, this is clearly a very different matter from keeping an army supplied against active opposition.

In view of the shifting balance between offense and defense, the ideal form of waging war will be to take the attack strategically while tactically staying on the defensive; in other words, a return to Moltke's technique of seizing such positions as will compel the enemy to counterattack. Since wars, however, take place not on some imaginary featureless plain but over real terrain whose main thoroughfares at least are usually well-known and, consequently, well guarded, this has always been much easier to say than to carry out. The result of all these facts will be to place a new premium on aggression, that is on being the first to strike before the other side is ready. Given the power of the defense and the consequent tendency toward stalemate, success must turn on the ability to win the war, or at least to make the greatest possible gains, in one mighty blow; conversely, an advantage once gained will be exceedingly difficult to cancel out again. In order to be capable of meeting these conditions, armies must be organized in such a way as to be capable of being hurled at each other at a moment's notice like ballistic missiles.[58] Strategic surprise, in the sense of seizing the initiative and being the first to deliver a blow, will be of the greatest importance. A glance at the frequency and shattering power of such blows in the last 35 years—the German offensive against Russia in 1947, Pearl

Harbor, the North Korean advance of 1950, the lightning-like Israeli attack of 1967, and of course the Arab attack of October 6, 1973—at once makes it clear that, as compared to previous periods, something has happened to make such offensives both more feasible and effective.[59] The speed and range of modern weapons systems; the centralization of command made possible by improved means of communication; the difficulties placed in the way of intelligence services that suffer from a deluge of information with which they are unable to cope; all these seem to have made strategic surprise much more effective and easy to achieve. True, in every case except 1967, the side that launched the initial attack ended up by losing the war; this, however, was made possible only by the most intensive effort, often lasting for years. Given the new power of the defense, the task is likely to become even harder in the future.

In summing up this section, the chief fact to note is that, while the "concentrated essence" of strategy—principles so general as to be almost meaningless—may be eternally valid, other strategic issues are at least partly dependent on technological and tactical factors and therefore subject to change. Annihilation versus attrition; offense versus defense; internal versus external lines; these and others are meaningful strategic concepts the balance between which will go a long way toward determining the character of any specific war. While it is true that military factors form only a small fraction of all the relevant considerations that make up strategy, these factors are nevertheless bound to assert themselves over a more or less long period of time in the form of trends. Insofar as these trends can be discerned—always a major problem of contemporary history—the Yom Kippur War would, on balance, seem to be leading us away from the "Third Armored Period," as the cycle beginning in 1917 has been called, toward new but ever-recurring forms of warfare.

IV. PERSPECTIVES

Though this study is concerned primarily with the military lessons of the Yom Kippur War, it should not be allowed to end without saying a word about the probable effects of those lessons on the wider, nonmilitary aspects of war and policy. This, to be sure, is an extremely difficult field where the number and importance of factors specific to each time and place loom larger than anywhere else; nevertheless, since grand strategy is at least partly dictated by military considerations, some conclusions can be drawn here.

One of the most outstanding facts about the Yom Kippur War was, surely, the enormous rate of attrition suffered by the participants. To give but a single example of the magnitude of the numbers involved, the total count of tanks lost on both sides must have approached 3,000 (75 percent of which were Arab) —and this in a conflict that did not last for quite three weeks. The figure is not only much larger than any that ever emerged from a comparable period of time in history;[60] it represents fully one-third of all the tanks that the members of NATO—France included—can muster. While details about the rates of consumption and attrition of other items are hard to come by, it is a fact of the greatest significance that both sides in the Middle East war found themselves beginning to run out of ammunition after a single week of murderous but indecisive fighting. And yet, as against their size and GNP, the belligerents were by no means ill-prepared; on the contrary, they are probably the most heavily-armed states on earth whose military establishments on land and in the air will bear comparison with those of second-rank powers such as France or Britain. If the war nevertheless threatened to "shut down" because of sheer lack of materiel, this reflected not unpreparedness but the fact that, at a time when technological progress has made decisive victories much harder to achieve, rates of consumption and attrition are necessarily pushed upward; in this respect, as in so many others, the Yom Kippur War has compelled a return from the cloud-cuckoo land of quick, cheap victories to the harsh realities of the last years of World War II or even World War I.

Though the war may have presented good news to NATO insofar as it demonstrated the superiority of most Western weapons[61] and the new possibilities opened up to the defense, it has also put a big question mark against the Alliance's ability to wage anything but the shortest of conventional wars. Certainly, rates of attrition cannot be expected to be any less high in a war in Europe; and it would be a tragedy not merely for the West but for mankind if NATO, after holding its own tactically, were to be faced with the choice of either surrendering or initiating a nuclear exchange because of insufficient reserves. As things stand at present, there is every reason to believe that there is only one group of states left in the world still capable of waging a sustained, full-scale conventional war—the Warsaw Pact.[62]

While NATO, comprising the richest—in any case, the most advanced—nations on earth still possesses the resources at least to prepare for more than the briefest of armed clashes, this is no longer true for most, if not all, other countries. For them, the superiority of the defense and the rates of attrition this imposes means that waging conventional war is simply ceasing to be a feasible option. As the Indo-Pakistani and Arab-Israeli conflicts clearly demonstrated, it will in the future be sheer lunacy for any state except the two superpowers—and if things go on as they do at present, for any except the Soviet Union alone[63]—to engage in a military adventure on any scale without making sure first of a resupply of ammunition and materiel that, again, only the superpowers and no other state can furnish. This, needless to say, will give the United States and the Soviet Union a new and unprecedently powerful lever to control the policy of their clients. If events in the Middle East have demonstrated the inability of the superpowers to prevent the outbreak of local wars, they have given even better proof of their ability to regulate not merely the extent and duration but also the intensity of those wars. Taps on, taps off; this, and not the action or inaction of the marionettes down the pipeline, will determine the shape of any future war.

Finally, should it prove impossible to make use of strategy in order to go around the new tactical obstacles facing tank and airplane; the shifting balance between offense and defense will affect the face of war in another, more profound way. It is one of the clichés of our time that, under modern conditions, war-making capability and the other constituents of society—its demographic, economic, and political power—are inescapably linked together as never before; hence, that it is the totality of a state's forces and not its military instrument alone that wins or loses wars. While the thesis as a whole is undoubtedly sound, it nevertheless appears to be more so for some kinds of modern wars than for others. In World War I, the superiority of the defense over the attack quickly nullified whatever qualitative advantage any army may have enjoyed and led to years of sustained fighting that finally ended in the victory of the side whose aggregate resources were the larger; in the early years of World War II, as in 1967, the superiority—even if only relative and temporary—of attack over defense enabled Germany and Israel to win some of the most smashing military victories of all time which, moreover, were gained by their respective forces-in-being *without* requiring mobilization in depth and *before* the full resources—especially nonmilitary—of the belligerents could be brought to bear.[64] Nor, indeed, is this consideration of the factors that affect the relationship between war and policy in its broadest sense limited to modern times only; looking at history as a whole, it appears that while a powerful tactical offense has frequently been associated with "limited" war,[65] the predominance of the defense has usually led to total commitment and total war.[66] Thus, whatever the exact course of the next Arab-Israeli fighting bout, there is every reason to believe that the days of "victory through limited liability" are fast running out; that the wars, even the conventional ones, of the future will become more, rather than less, total, subjecting the resources of the societies waging them to an ever increasing drain and strain. If it is true that the totalization of war in this sense was co-responsible for its barbarization (see Falls, 1961: ch. VIII, esp. 147-151), nothing but more terror and barbarism can be expected in the bargain. It is a daunting prospect.

NOTES

1. Early in the Yom Kippur War it was widely believed that the Arab armies had undergone a radical quantitative improvement. However, the quality of troops always reflects the educational and social infrastructure of the nation they belong to, which in this case hardly changed much; and the Arabs had always been good on the defensive and in "set piece" battles. For some instructive comments see Young (1967: 112).

2. Original Hebrew title of Teveth's book (1969).

3. For accounts of the battle see Young (1967: 103-106); Marshall (1967: 41-52); and O'Ballance (1972: 102-118). For a recent and overcritical Israeli view see Amidror (1974).

4. This is admirably illustrated by the "typical" Napoleonic battle in which skirmishers were used for the initial clash; cannon, infantry in column formation, and cuirassiers for the main action; and light cavalry for mopping up and exploitation.

5. A good example of this kind of conservatism is World War I, which saw masses of tightly-packed troops being repeatedly sent into the muzzles of hostile machine guns.

6. For the resemblance between medieval and armored warfare see Fuller (1943).

7. The similarities and differences between the two formations are discussed in Oman (1963: 76, 106).

8. Here used to mean the art of using one's military resources in attaining one's aim.

9. Nevertheless, ranges did close down sufficiently to require new weapons; accordingly, the last years of World War I saw the introduction of the submachine gun.

10. A good example is the Macedonian phalanx of the third and second centuries B.C., beaten by the Roman legions at Cynoscephalae (197) and Pydna (168).

11. A close parallel, however, is the Second Battle of Alamein. Thanks are due to Lieutenant Kadish Allon for pointing this out to me.

12. Sadat's expression to Achbar al Yom editor Mussa Tsabri (Sadat, 1974).

13. An Egyptian (or Soviet) army is equivalent to a Western corps.

14. The estimates vary between 1,750 (Insight Team, 1973: 241) and 2,500 (Zahal spokesman); the estimate of the International Institute for Strategic Studies (1974: 26) is 2,000. Of this force, 700 to 1,200 tanks are said to have crossed to the east side.

15. The mountainous southern half is virtually impassable to troop movements.

16. For part of this analysis of the Egyptian offensive I am indebted to Dr. Amnon Selah (1974).

17. While some observers have attributed this fact to sheer Egyptian incompetence (Marshall, 1973: 10-12), the real reason may have been more complex. It appears that Egyptian COS Mohamed Shazli wanted to exploit success, especially that won by the Third Army in the south, in order to advance deeper into the Sinai, but was restrained by Defense Minister Ismail. Whether this stemmed from Ismail's preference for a "set piece" battle (Insight Team, 1973: 112), from fear of going out of range of cover, or from the hope of making the IDF wear itself out in futile counter-attacks, we do not know.

18. Throughout the war, the Egyptian air force is supposed to have flown only some 2,500 sorties, and most of these were flown in the last days of the war in a desperate attempt to stop the IDF from encircling the Egyptian Third Army. See Aviation Week (1973).

19. Since we do not know the scenario of a future war as envisaged by the Israeli General Staff, there is no way of assessing the role of the Bar Lev Line in it. The IDF seems to have worked on the assumption that reserves would not be immediately available and evolved a plan to hold an eventual Egyptian crossing with their regular forces alone; this plan, according to such officers as former COS Haim Bar Lev, Major General Dan Lanner, and Major Ezer Weizmann, was simply not carried out.

20. It was for this that Gonen was subsequently removed (Agranat Report, 1974).

21. For the role of the ramparts see Sadat (1974).

22. Exactly what forces were involved is not clear. Initially it was claimed that an entire Israeli brigade (the 190th) had been annihilated, but this does not tally with the fact that the captured commander of this unit, Asaf Yaguri, was a lieutenant colonel and thus by right a battalion commander. It seems, however, that while the destruction of Yaguri's battalion received the most publicity other forces were also involved.

23. The main weapons were two: the RPG-7 antitank rifle and, above all, the Sagger antitank guided missile. Both are essentially infantry weapons, though the Sagger can be and has been mounted atop vehicles.

24. There has been some doubt as to how far the Syrians intended to advance. The full facts, of course, are unknown, but the participation of a large number of amphibious vehicles in the Syrian assault makes one inclined to think that they did not plan to stop at the pre-1967 armistice lines.

25. The main weapons of this kind in the Israeli arsenal were French SS-10 and SS-11 guided antitank missiles and 76 mm. recoilless rifles mounted on jeeps. Both were obsolete and were, in any case, available in limited quantities only.

26. This was due to several factors, including: a. better training, giving greater accuracy and a much more rapid rate of fire; b. better range-finding equipment on Israel's Western tanks; c. superior ammunition, especially with regard to accuracy at long range; d. the fact that Israeli tank guns could be depressed further than Arab ones, enabling them to make superior use of cover. For a popular but thorough survey of the factors that count in this kind of warfare, see Macksey (1972).

27. Israel, however, lost 60 to 80 planes during the first week of the war, and most of those went down over the Syrian front. See Aviation Week (1973) for a breakdown of the figures.

28. The figures move between 600 (International Institute of Strategic Studies, 1974: 26) to 1,300 (Dayan, 1974a).

29. Since the Jordanians had no air defense system at all comparable to the Syrian one, such a movement would have little to fear from counterattack on its right. In the opinion of Major General (Ret.) Mattityahu Peled, a thrust of this kind might have cut Syria off from Jordan, launched a rear attack on the Syrians, and changed the political map of the region by linking up with the Druze population in Syria.

30. Mainly SAM-2 and SAM-3 missiles, which, in contrast to the SAM-6 and SAM-7, are not very mobile. For details about the Egyptian air defenses, see the New York Times (1973b: 16) and Flight International (1974: 845).

31. Figure mentioned by Major General Haim Herzog (1974). Israeli losses are said to have amounted to six tanks.

32. Since no power would sell Israel bridging equipment, the IDF developed its own.

33. For detailed descriptions of the battle see Bamahaneh (1974) and Yedi'oth Aharonoth (1974).

34. President Sadat did not seem to be aware of the crossing when he spoke to the People's Assembly on the morning of October 16. For this ignorance the overcentralization of the Egyptian command system has been blamed.

35. In theory, the Israelis could have gone either west to Cairo or north to encircle the Egyptian Second Army. Political and logistic considerations seem to have ruled the first alternative out of the question, whereas the second option would have faced the difficult terrain north of the Great Bitter Lake, which is cut by many shallow irrigation ditches. In opting for the southern direction, the Israelis also enjoyed the advantage of having their left flank protected by the Bitter Lake.

36. After the IAF had failed to destroy the canal bridges in the first two days of the war, it concentrated on the Golan front and left the Sinai virtually without air support.

37. In fact, Egyptian use of the RPG-7 antitank rifle in the Yom Kippur War was suicidal, and the troops employing it were dubbed "throwaway soldiers" in Israel.

38. See Senator Tom Eagleton's comments (1974) concerning the American M-60 main battle tank.

39. The best recent discussion of these problems is Ogorkiewicz (1973: 754-758).

40. "If I only had more artillery!" Gonen is supposed to have exclaimed on the evening of October 6.

41. Whereas the Egyptians are presently buying Lynx helicopters from Britain, the Israelis are receiving Huey cobras from the United States.

42. See Note 27. It should also be noted that the IAF's losses were largely due to a conscious decision to sacrifice aircraft by having them operate against tactical targets in close support before the air defenses had been cleared away as had been planned.

43. Laser and television-guided standoff bombs are likely to be very effective indeed against fixed air defense installations; their effect against the more mobile systems that played such a prominent role in the Yom Kippur War, however, remains to be seen.

44. For good accounts of warfare in this period see Spaulding et al. (1924) and Oman (1957).

45. Alternatively, it should be possible to exploit the weakness of present-day antitank missiles by advancing to within point-blank range; for this purpose, however, IFVs may well prove more suitable than tanks.

46. This is the Soviet concept; see Erickson (1971: 75).

47. This seems to have been one of the principal lessons Israel drew from the war; see Gur (1974).

48. For example, Liddell Hart's six "positive" and two "negative" principles laid down as "the concentrated essence of strategy" in his book, Strategy (1954: 347-351).

49. The most systematic exposition of the two kinds of strategy is still Delbrück (1890).

50. The best short summary of the issue is Erfurth (1939: 52-58).

51. Thus, Washington took 15 days to march 200 miles from the Hudson to the Chesapeake; in 1805, Napoleon's army covered 375 miles from the Channel Coast to the Rhine in 26 days; and Sherman took 50 days to march 425 miles from Savannah to Goldsboro. Patton needed 38 days to "race" 400 miles across France in 1944, and the pace was not increased when the Eighth Army pursued from the Naktong to the Ch'ongchon in the autumn of 1950.

52. For a thorough exposition see Addington (1971), especially chapters VIII and IX.

53. In another sense, however, its effects were only too apparent, for the limited mobility of their air defenses is likely to have played a crucial role in the shaping of Arab strategy.

54. There remains, of course, the problem of surface-to-surface missiles. Exactly what their effect will be nobody knows, but barring the

use of nuclear warheads it is likely to be less, rather than more, than that of manned aircraft.

55. The best examples are Rommel's defenses at El Alamein and Normandy.

56. Had it not been for the Luftwaffe's undisputed mastery of the sky, even the French of 1940 might have severed the thin German armored thrust reaching to the English Channel at its joint.

57. For the Yom Kippur War, see International Institute for Strategic Studies (1974); for a more general discussion, see Heilbrunn (1967: 97 ff.).

58. This is one of the main lessons of the war, now being applied by both sides in the Middle East.

59. As against this, see Clausewitz's dictum that surprise attacks seldom succeed to any *remarkable* (original emphasis) extent (Clausewitz, 1962). Here, clearly, the master has become outdated.

60. The closest parallel is probably the Battle of Kursk in 1943.

61. The T-54 and T-55, mainstays of the Arab (and Warsaw Pact) armored corps, are now definitely out of date. The T-62 did better, though it is hard to form an exact idea of its worth because of the immense qualitative edge of the IDF's tankmen, who were sometimes able to successfully use World War II Shermans against the most recent Soviet equipment. The Sagger antitank missile is good, but less so than those now being produced in Europe and the United States. In the F-4 Phantom, the IAF possessed a plane that, for all the great speed of recent Soviet models, is still unsurpassed in versatility and all-around capability. The SAM-6 probably came out to better advantage than any other Soviet weapon system. All in all, however, the problems of Western arms result less from their quality than from the limited quantities in which they are available.

62. Paradoxically, it is Soviet military doctrine that has always envisaged the next war in Europe as nuclear from the outset, whereas it is Western doctrine that foresees the possibility of a war that, initially at least, will remain conventional.

63. In a war lasting for three weeks, Israel—a nation of less than three million people—lost more tanks than the United States produces in a year. To resupply this and other kinds of equipment, the United States, allegedly the largest power on earth, had to scrape bottom. See the report on discussions between Henry Kissinger and a group of Jewish intellectuals (New York Times, 1973a); see also Aviation Week (1974) and Special Subcommittee on the Middle East of the Committee of Armed Services, House of Representatives (1973: 3).

64. See the brilliant analysis of the grand-strategic ideas behind the Blitzkrieg concept in Milward (1964: ch. I, esp. 7 ff.).

65. Limited in scale, intensity, and time; see the interesting remarks in Nickerson (1940: 366 ff.).

66. This was as true in the 1550s (following the widespread introduction of "Italian" style fortification and the bastion) as it was in 1914-1918 and 1942-1945.

REFERENCES

ADCOCK, F. E. (1957) The Greek and Macedonian Art of War. Berkeley and Los Angeles: Univ. of California Press.
ADDINGTON, L. H. (1971) The Blitzkrieg Era and the German General Staff, 1865-1941. New Brunswick: Rutgers Univ. Press.
Agranat Inquiry Committee's Report (1974) Printed in Ma'ariv (April 3).
AMIDROR, B. (1974) Article in Yedi'oth Aharonot (June 5).
Aviation Week (1974) Article on Phantom Planes (May 13).
--- (1973) Article (December 3).
Bamahaneh (1974) Article (April 17).
BROWN, N. (1963) Strategic Mobility. London: Chatto & Windus.
CHANDLER, D. G. (1966) The Campaigns of Napoleon. New York: Macmillan.
CLAUSEWITZ, C. (1962) On War. London: K. Paul.
DAYAN, M. (1974a) Statement to Yedi'oth Aharonoth (September 22).
--- (1974b) Closed press conference of October 9, 1973, as reported in Ma'ariv (February 15).
DELBRUCK, H. (1890) Die Strategic des Perikles erlaeutert durch die Strategic Friedrick des Grossen. Berlin: G. Reimer.
EAGLETON, T. (1974) Comments reported in Jerusalem Post (February 8).
ELAZAR, D. (1973) Press conference (October 8).
ERFURTH, W. (1939) Die Vernichtungssieg. Berlin: E. S. Mittler.
ERICKSON, J. (1971) Soviet Military Power. London: Royal United Service Institute for Defense Studies.
FALLS, C. (1961) The Art of War. London: Oxford V.P.
Flight International (1974) Article (June 27).
FULLER, J.F.C. (1962) The Conduct of War, 1789-1961. London.
--- (1945) Armament and History. New York: Scribner's.
--- (1943) Armoured Warfare. London: Eyre & Spottiswoode.
--- (1936a) The Dragon's Teeth. London: Constable & Co.
--- (1936b) 1917 memorandum, quoted in Memoirs of an Unconventional Soldier. London: Nicholson & Watson.
GUDERIAN, H. (1967) Panzer Leader. New York: Ballantine.
GUR, M. (1974) Television interview (September 29).
HART, B.H.L. (1960) Deterrent or Defense. London: Stevens.
--- (1954) Strategy. London: F. A. Praeger.
HEILBRUNN, O. (1967) Conventional Warfare in the Nuclear Age. London: Allen & Unwin.

HERZOG, H. (1974) Television talk (September 26).
HOWARD, M. (1961) The Franco-Prussian War: the German Invasion of 1870-1871. London: R. Hart Davies.
Insight Team of the Sunday Times (1973) Insight on the Middle East War. London: André Deutsch.
International Defense Review (1973, December).
International Institute for Strategic Studies (1974) Strategic Survey 1973. London: IISS.
LOT, F. (1946) L'art Militaire et les Armes du Moyen Age. Paris: Payot.
MACKSEY, K. (1972) Tank: Fact and Feats. London: Macdonald.
MARSHALL, S.L.A. (1973) Article in the New Leader (November 12).
--- (1967) Swift Sword. New York: American Heritage.
MIKSCHE, F. O. (1971) "Mobility-kill in der Grenzverteidigung. Ist der Panzer tot eine Studie." Wehr und Wirtschaft (August 7).
--- (1944) Blitzkrieg. London: Harmondsworth.
MILWARD, A. (1964) The German Economy at War. London: Athlone Press.
New York Times (1973a) Article (December 6).
--- (1973b) Article (October 19).
NICKERSON, H. (1940) The Armed Horde. New York: G. P. Putnam.
O'BALLANCE, E. (1972) The Third Arab-Israeli War. London: Faber & Faber.
OMAN, C.W.C. (1963) The Art of War in the Middle Ages. New York: Cornell Univ. Press.
--- (1957) The Art of War in the Sixteenth Century. London: Methuen.
ORGILL, D. (1970) The Tank: Studies in the Development and Use of a Weapon. London: Heinemann.
OGORKIEWICZ, R. (1973) "The next generation of battle tanks." International Defense Review (December): 754-758.
SADAT, A. (1974) Quoted in Ma'ariv (September 13).
SELAH, A. (1974) "Soviet doctrine and Arab performance." Jerusalem Post Magazine (February 8).
SHARON, A. (1973) Interview to the New York Times (November 12).
SMART, I. (1973) Article in The Times (October 24).
SPAULDING, O. L. et al. (1924) Warfare: A Study of Military Methods from the Earliest Times. London: G. G. Harrap.
Special Subcommittee on the Middle East of the Committee of Armed Services, House of Representatives (1973) Report (December 13).
TEVETH, S. (1969) The Tanks of Tamuz. New York: Viking Press.
WINTRINGHAM, T. (1943) Weapons and Tactics. London: Faber & Faber.
YADIN, Y. (1954) "For by wise counsel thou shalt make thy war," pp. 386-404 in B. H. Liddell Hart, Strategy. New York: F. A. Praeger.
Yedi'oth Aharonoth (1974) Article (September 24).
YOUNG, P. (1967) The Israeli Campaign 1967. London: W. Kimber.

ISRAEL-EGYPT AGREEMENT
on the Separation of Forces
18 January 1974

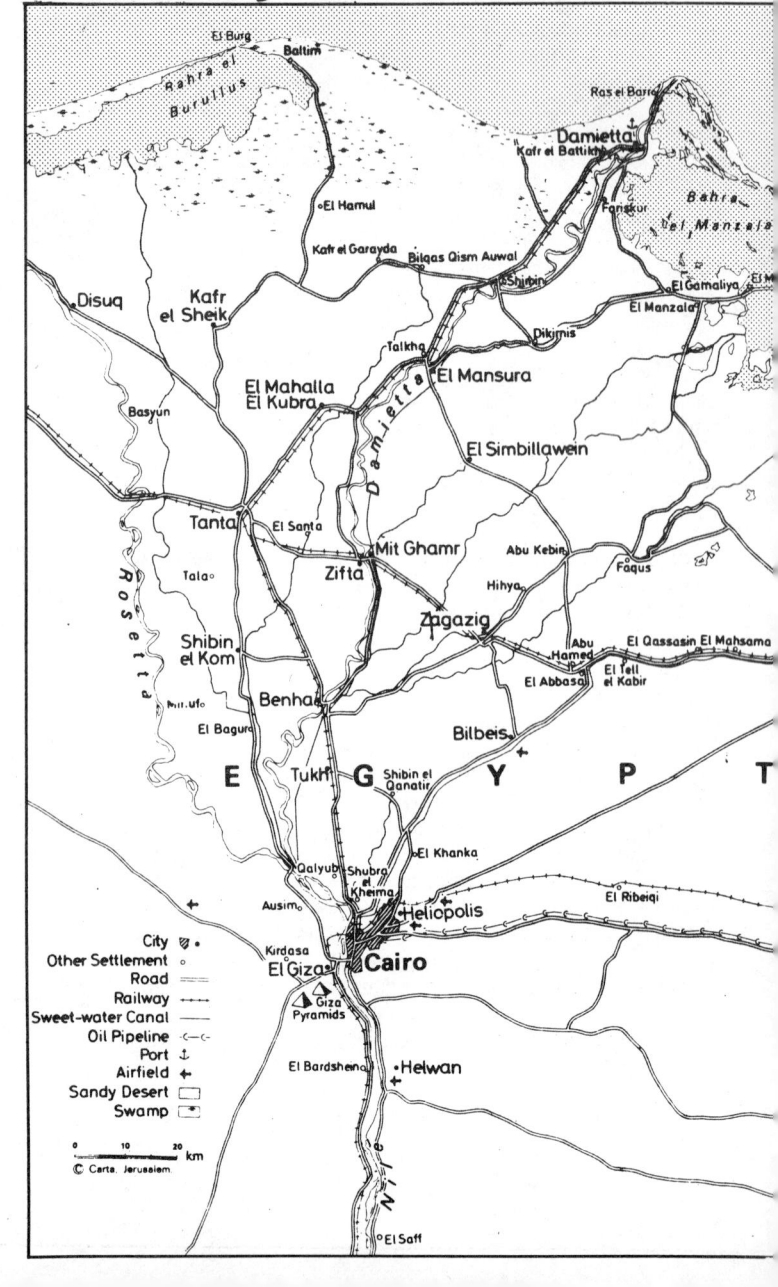

Designations A, B, C are explained in The Agreement (page 60)

Reproduced by permission of Carta Cartographers and Publishers, Jerusalem, Israel.

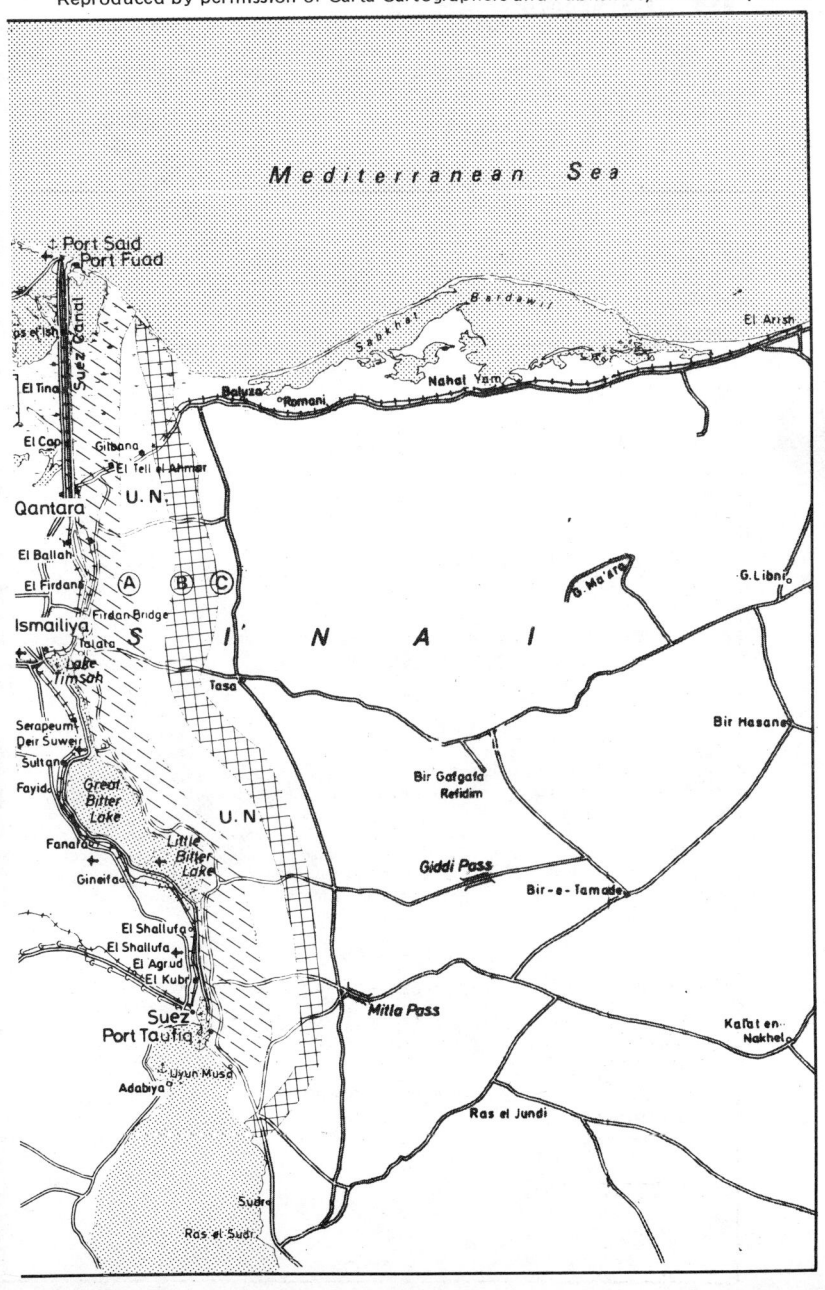

THE AGREEMENT

A

Egypt and Israel will scrupulously observe the cease-fire on land, sea and air called for by the U.N. Security Council and will refrain from the time of the signing of this document from all military or para-military actions against each other.

B

The military forces of Egypt and Israel will be separated in accordance with the following principles:

1. All Egyptian forces on the east side of the Canal will be redeployed west of the line designated as line A on the attached map. All Israeli forces, including those west of the Suez Canal and the Bitter Lakes, will be deployed east of the line designated as line B on the attached map.

2. The area between the Egyptian and Israeli lines will be a zone of disengagement in which the United Nations Emergency Force (Unef) will be stationed. Unef will continue to consist of units from countries that are not permanent members of the Security Council.

3. The area between the Egyptian line and the Suez Canal will be limited in armament and forces.

4. The area between the Israeli line (line B on the attached map) and the line designated as line C on the attached map, which runs along the western base of the mountains where the Gidi and Mitla passes are located, will be limited in armament and forces.

5. The limitations referred to in paragraphs 3 and 4 will be inspected by Unef. Existing procedures of the Unef, including the attaching of Egyptian and Israeli liaison officers to Unef, will be continued.

6. Air forces of the two sides will be permitted to operate up to their respective lines without interference from the other side.

C

The detailed implementation of the disengagement of forces will be worked out by military representatives of Egypt and Israel who will agree on the stages of this process. These representatives will meet no later than 48 hours after the signature of this agreement at Kilometre 101 under the aegis of the United Nations for this purpose.

They will complete this task within five days. Disengagement will begin within 48 hours after the completion of the work of the military representatives and in no event later than seven days after the signature of this agreement. The process of disengagement will be completed not later than 40 days after it begins.

D

This agreement is not regarded by Egypt and Israel as a final peace agreement. It constitutes a first step toward a final, just and durable peace according to the provisions of Security Council Resolution 338 and within the framework of the Geneva conference.